Designing the Life of Your Dreams from the Outside In

Designing the Life of Your Dreams from the Outside In

✦

Easy to apply tips for any space utilizing feng shui and healthy home principles to help facilitate your life's goals

DeAnna Radaj

iUniverse, Inc.
New York Lincoln Shanghai

Designing the Life of Your Dreams from the Outside In

Easy to apply tips for any space utilizing feng shui and healthy home principles to help facilitate your life's goals

iUniverse books may be ordered through booksellers or by contacting:

iUniverse
2021 Pine Lake Road, Suite 100
Lincoln, NE 68512
www.iuniverse.com
1-800-Authors (1-800-288-4677)

ISBN-13: 978-0-595-39979-6 (pbk)
ISBN-13: 978-0-595-84367-1 (ebk)
ISBN-10: 0-595-39979-7 (pbk)
ISBN-10: 0-595-84367-0 (ebk)

Printed in the United States of America

This book could not have been done without the love and support of many people.

Cristina, you helped "open" my writer's block and helped to inspire me again!

Deb and Renee, you are 2 of my biggest cheerleaders and always ready, willing and able to try new ideas for classes and workshops! You are the ultimate guinea pigs!!! Thank you!

Corrine, thanks for the time, effort and support in getting this project finished.

Marg, you are one of my dearest friends. Thank you for that and for always being ready to throw my own words back at me. (I give great advice, hey?)

And finally, to my Mom, who is the most important person in my life. I appreciate all of your support and the fact that you have never let me quit. (You're also an awesome "puppy nanny"!). I love you.

Contents

1

Introduction

Feng Shui. Sustainable design. Off-gassing. Environmental sensitivities. These words and phrases can be scary and intimidating to those that aren't familiar with "design lingo." This book is designed to easily incorporate these terms into your every day vocabulary or at the very least, make them less intimidating. It will identify simple ways for you to incorporate sound design principles into your home, work space and/or lifestyle and will make you the envy of all your friends, as they enter your beautiful, calming and (more importantly) healthy home.

Feng Shui, the Chinese art of placement, has been around for over 5000 years. It has gained popularity in the USA in the past 10 years and interior designers, architects and real estate agents are using its principles. Feng Shui, at its most basic level, is about living in harmony with your surrounding environment. Its concepts include gaining an understanding of the five elements: Fire, Water, Earth, Metal and Wood, and how these elements work productively and destructively. It is identifying what is important in your life (goal-setting and prioritizing) and applying those practices to the nine life areas (Career/Life Aspirations, Knowledge/Spirituality, Family, Wealth/Abundance, Success/Fame/Luck, Relationships, Creativity/Kids, Travel/Helpful People and Health/Well-Being) that are illustrated by the I Ching and the Bagua board.

****Good Design is Not Necessarily Good Feng Shui. Good Feng Shui is ALWAYS Good Design.* ***

In conducting workshops and seminars across the country, I've developed a "top 10" list of practical design tips that includes feng shui principles that the feng shui "impaired" can easily and quickly understand and apply, basic Design 101 theory, and the evils of mental and physical clutter. This list will give you the tools you need to design or re-design any space in a healthy way with consideration of all occupants and one that is aesthetically pleasing. Clutter is discussed in

1

detail because of its implications not only with respect to the physical aspects of your space, but also with consideration of the mental clutter everyone carries around in the form of emotional baggage. From a pure design standpoint, if you can't see the floor or built-in focal points of a room (picture a fireplace that's blocked with boxes,) you can't expect to realize the full potential of a room or recognize what you or a paid designer have to work with. From a psychological standpoint, why do you keep gifts from exes or clothes that are too old or don't fit? Don't you want to make room for new things (opportunities or people) in your life? If you don't use it, need it or love it-GET RID OF IT!

*** *To keep doing the same thing, (re)acting and living in the same way and expecting different results is a sign of insanity.* ***

While researching stories for various articles and my workshops, I have found the correlation between our physical environments and our health (mental, spiritual and physical) amazing. We have all heard of "sick building" syndrome, how the buildings we work and live in can actually make us physically ill, and the effect they can have on workplace productivity. But do you realize that through more conscientious and educated choices regarding your purchasing habits you can counteract these effects?

The GREEN movement has recently become mainstream. There is a rise in LEED certified buildings throughout the country. All natural and organic food/cleaners are now available in large grocery store chains, and health care is paying more attention to causes, and not just the symptoms, of illness. They are taking alternative medicine more seriously as well. This is cause for great hope. Five years ago, you would have been laughed out of a home building supply chain (or at the very least looked at cross-eyed) if you asked for "no VOC" paint. Now every major paint manufacturer makes a "healthy" paint in a variety of color choices. After applying these tips, you will notice a difference in air quality, how you sleep at night and your general well-being after putting into effect some of these simple changes.

*** *Without your health, nothing else can matter or bring you joy.* ***

I hope you enjoy the following chapters and gain a greater knowledge of how your environment truly makes a difference in you mentally and physically. After reading this book, you will see you don't have to raze your home and start from scratch (many of us don't have the luxury of building from the ground up,) but you can change your buying habits, make simple changes to your existing space-plan, color scheme and "collecting" habits and create the life, and home, of your dreams!

2

The (Abridged) History of Feng Shui

Literally translated, feng shui means "wind and water." Feng shui was actually started as a way to identify or select auspicious gravesites in China over 5,000 years ago. It was thought that the better the position of the gravesite, the better the fortunes of the remaining family members. Many schools of thought regarding feng shui principles have surfaced over the years, and it is because of this that there is so much confusion. What direction should the door face? Where is the relationship area? Where do I put a crystal? No mirrors in the bedroom? Ahhhhhhh!

First and foremost, knowing which school you are dealing with and whether you are comfortable with that philosophy will make the biggest difference when designing your space. Once you know that, you are ready to begin. It should be noted that the following are very brief descriptions of the various schools.

The first school of thought, and considered to be the oldest, is the Form school. The Form school takes into consideration all geographical formations in and around the area where a building is being built. A great example is the "armchair" analogy. The best place to build is in the "seat" of the chair. The area behind the building shoud be as high or higher than your building, like a backrest. This can be accomplished with tree placement if there is nothing located behind your house. This is a psychologically secure position. The sides, or armrests, should be no higher than your building and ideally a little smaller. This is for protection on the sides, but you can still ideally see over them. The front of the space should be clear and clutter-free. Here you want to be able to see anyone approaching. There should be no large obstructions blocking your view. This includes trees, fences or other buildings (i.e. garage, shed, etc...)

The next school is the Compass school. This is the school most thought of when feng shui is mentioned. Picture an old Chinese man with a compass pointing in various directions. This compass can identify where your couch goes and on what diagonal the desk should be placed. This school uses a compass called a Lo-pan to correctly determine the degree of the direction that is the most auspicious, or best, location for a particular room or piece of furniture. There are various calculations that are used in this school that are based on the date of birth of the occupants and the "birth" (can be construction date or date you moved in) of the house. Based on these calculations, you can derive your personal auspicious numbers or "pa-kua" numbers. These numbers relate to the directions in a positive or "inauspicious" way. The basis or principle here is to take advantage of or maximize your good/positive directions. This is accomplished by facing and benefiting from the "good" energy that you will receive while keeping your back to the bad or inauspicious energy.

Finally, there is the Black Hat Sect school of thought or Bagua School. Bagua is translated to "eight-sided figure" or octagon shaped. This figure is then divided into segments, like a pie, with a center piece-giving you nine areas. These nine areas are assigned different life areas. They are: Career/Life Path, Knowledge/ Spirituality, Family, Wealth/Abundance, Success/Fame/Luck, Relationships, Creativity/Kids, Helpful People/Travel, and Health/Well-Being.

The bottom tier (Knowledge/Spirituality, Career/Life Path, and Helpful People/ Travel) should always be lined up with the entryway wall of your building floor plan or the individual room you are working on. Then you can super-impose the Bagua over the floor plan and see what "areas" need to be worked on, or what areas you'd like to work on. Once you get the concept of the Bagua and how to properly line up the grid, you will be able to work on any space and be able to identify the corresponding life area.

These life areas can be "activated" by using the element, color, shape, item or direction that is associated with that life area (i.e. relationship-hearts.) See below:

Wealth/Abundance	*Success/Fame*	*Relationships*
Purple/Metallic	Red	Red/Pink/Peach
Water Element	Fire Element	Earth Element
Wavy lines	Triangle	Squares
SE	S	SW

Family	*Health/Well-Being*	*Creativity/Kids*
Green	Yellow/Earth-tones	White/Metallic
Wood Element	Earth Element	Metal Element
Rectangle	Squares	Circles
E	Center	W

Knowledge/Spirituality	*Career/Life Path*	*Helpful People/Travel*
Blue	Black	Gray
Earth Element	Water Element	Metal Element
Squares	Wavy Lines	Circles
NE	N	NW

As you can see, each school of thought has a different approach. Read up in more detail on each school to see which one you are more comfortable with. Once you have established this, you will be able to choose books that are applicable to your interest and be better able to find the proper advice. You can find feng shui practioners in your local Yellow Pages or on the Internet. Some interior designers and architects are also versed in feng shui. Books are available at all major book retailers, Amazon.com and BarnesandNoble.com. Type in "feng shui" into the search engine and see what pops up.

3

Why We Need the Top 10 List

The Top 10 List was created in response to my beginning Feng Shui class where we ended the class with a summary of easy to apply tips that incorporated feng shui and healthy home principles that anyone could apply to any space.

The Top 10 List is:

1. Eliminate Clutter.
2. Utilize the Power Position of the room.
3. Utilize the 5 senses and the 5 elements in your design plan.
4. Bring the Outdoors in.
5. Maintain a Welcoming, unobstructed entryway.
6. Bathroom design and how it relates to your wealth.
7. Create a personal sanctuary.
8. Maintain a smooth traffic pattern throughout the space.
9. Don't be afraid to be CREATIVE and try something "out of the box."
10. Detoxify your space.

This book will explain these principles in a conversational and easy to apply format. It will also describe why the principles brought forth are important and how to apply them to your space. It should be noted that any of the changes you make to your home, no matter how small, will make a difference to you, your family and your space.

Life is stressful enough. Don't allow your home to be another source of stress. Our homes are our refuge and sanctuary from the outside and an expression of our personality. Don't be afraid to demonstrate that personality and make your home yours!

4

Clutter-Organizing Your Inner Pack Rat

Do you own your stuff or does your stuff own you? If you answered the later, this chapter is for you. Did you know that getting rid of our "stuff" is the #1 New Year's Resolution made every year? It's probably the first one to be broken as well. Our stuff wastes our time, in terms of maintaining, cleaning and searching for it. It wastes our money by us having to store it and/or buying duplicate items because we can't find what we're looking for and it's just easier to go out and buy a new one. It also causes a great deal of stress (see before-mentioned examples) if we let it. You can feel overwhelmed, blocked, embarrassed and even depressed. At times, you can even be financially disorganized as you lose track of bills, bank statements and other important paperwork. By hanging on to "this stuff," you are actually hanging on to emotional baggage, a security blanket if you will, or the past lifestyle that is associated with a particular item.

Clutter is defined as anything you don't use, need, want or love. Clutter is related to stagnant energy in the house and in your life. For example, do you still have all of your old high school trophies/medals/clothes on display? Are you still re-living the glory days of old instead of being present in your life today? If you don't use something, or if you don't need or even particularly want something and it doesn't make you happy or there is no positive association with an item…. Why do you keep it? We all keep items because we USED to like them or we paid a lot of money for them. There is a real fear associated with getting rid of an item-ANY ITEM. We are afraid that we won't be able to replace it, or that we are letting go of our past and associated memories or the all too familiar guilt.

Let's address the fear of replacing the item. First, why are you worried about replacing an item that you aren't using, want or like? Secondly, if you do need the item, chances are there is a new, improved and cheaper model available. Get rid of the old!

The second fear is one of the hardest to deal with, as there are frequently so many memories invested in some of our collectibles or "family heirlooms," it's the fear of forgetting the person or event that surrounds an item. That being said, there are some items that have extraordinary meaning-a pressed flower from a wedding bouquet, your first stuffed animal, the first card your child made in school…all things that can be kept and displayed for you to enjoy. However, EVERY card ever made by your child or EVERY stuffed animal ever bought does not qualify. Be selective. This fear really comes into play when dealing with the loss of a loved one. We fear that by getting rid of the departed one's personal belongings, we are in essence "getting rid" of that person from our memories, thoughts and hearts. This is not true-*Memories are in our hearts not our things!*

Lastly, do you feel guilty if you get rid of something? The item can be a piece of clothing, a knick-knack or an expensive gift. For example, I have a friend who was given a cashmere sweater by her then boyfriend. They broke up. She kept the sweater and continued to wear it. She would receive compliments on the sweater, but every time she wore the sweater or had to answer where she got the sweater, it made her think of her EX, bringing up all of the memories associated with him and their now ended relationship. She eventually stopped wearing the sweater because of all the bad memories associated with wearing it, but she wouldn't donate it, as "it was expensive." So to sum up, she kept an item that she used to like and whenever she wore or saw it, it brought up very intense negative emotions, but she wouldn't get rid of it because it was an expensive items. If something you have/own doesn't make you happy, why do you keep it? If you don't love it-get rid of it. By hanging on to old things/items, you are really hanging on to emotional baggage

OK so now you know what to look for or how you should feel when you start to go through and organize your belongings and collections, but HOW do you start. A quick three-step process follows:

1.   Give yourself permission to let go of things.

2.   Donate/sell/toss what you don't need, love or use.

3.   Organize what's left.

The first one is the hardest and is probably what stops people from even getting started in the process. It is OK to let things go and move forward. If your home and life are "cluttered," how can you experience growth and allow new things to enter your life. This can be in the form of new items or new relationships.

Clutter tends to accumulate at the front entrance, in the bathroom, on counter-tops and in closets, cars and purses. In feng shui terms, each area of the house corresponds to a different life area. Is there an area that you're having problems with? Is there an area where you'd like to see some sort of change to occur? Refer to the chart in Chapter 2 to see which life area is cluttered and how it currently applies to your life. Are your finances a mess? Are you having health issues? Do you start projects but never seem to finish them? Clear up the clutter and see what happens!

Dr Robert Baker, PhD, gives us seven tips to lead a clutter-free life:

1. Start small-a drawer, a closet, your purse…then the task isn't so daunting.

2. Evaluate your items one at a time-ask yourself if you really love, need, want or use the item. If the answer is NO to any of the above, get rid of it.

3. Sit down and make a list of what you really need and what you want. You'll be surprised at what you already have and what you have that you thought you needed. Do you really need more than one hair dryer? (When I did this I actually had 3 hair-dryers: one to use, the second one for an emergency in case the first one broke, and the other was for travel!)

4. Give yourself a homework assignment. Clean one drawer a day/week…this will give you a sense of accomplishment and will help to break down the overall task.

5. Get outside advice. Sometimes it's hard to be objective regarding certain items (i.e. clothes, collections…) It's OK to bring in a 3rd party, whether it's a friend, family member or a professional organizer. Remember to not take what they say personally, and that they are there to help you. You may get to return the favor!

6. Use existing storage. If you have too much stuff, it's easy to run out to the store and buy more storage containers. Instead of going out and

spending more money on something you don't need, utilize the storage and space that you currently have. You will be surprised at the end of this that you will have extra space and nothing to put there

7.   Stop before you buy anything else. ALWAYS ask yourself "why" you want to purchase the item. We tend to buy on want as opposed to need. If you decide that you do need the item, let go of one item you currently have to make room for the new item.

OK-you're all set to start purging your clutter. You need to set up three piles: keep, sell/donate, and toss. Remember your mantra-BE BRUTAL! If you are starting with a drawer, empty out the drawer. If you are starting with a closet, empty out the closet. Only put back what you LOVE, USE and WORKS. Period. These are your KEEP items.

Items to SELL/DONATE are things that you don't respond positively to in the above questions. Have a rummage sale; sell on eBay; put an ad in the paper. These are all effective ways to sell unwanted items. To sell an item, make sure it is still in usable condition, that all pieces work like they are supposed to and that the item is clean. Price accordingly. If you are selling a shirt that you wore in college 15 years ago, it's not worth the $20 you originally paid-try $1. The stuffed animal from your first boyfriend when you were 12-try $1. Are you getting the drift here? It's a rummage sale. Now, if you are trying to sell an antique or collectible, find out the fair market price from an antique dealer or on-line. EBay is probably your best bet for this. You can also try consignment shops. However, they will take a percentage of the sale and can be picky about the age of the item. Decide how much time you really want to spend on this. You must be prepared to toss or donate any items that don't sell.

If you decide that you just want the "stuff" out of your space, donating the item is your best bet. It's also a tax write-off, and you are helping out an organization and people who can use the help. Some charitable organizations will even pick up your items for you! There are many organizations to choose from: Salvation Army, Purple Heart, and Goodwill. These are some of the larger organizations, however, there are many other organizations that will take donations. Donate those books, toys, puzzles and games to a Ronald McDonald house, library, children's hospital or shelter for the homeless or abused and battered families. Check your Yellow Pages to see what's in your area and their policies.

Toss those things that are broken and can't be fixed, are ripped and/or torn or just junk that you've accumulated. Get a dumpster if you have to. After my father died, my Mom started what began as just clearing out some of my father's things into a one-year project that cleaned out the house from top to bottom. Literally, two dumpsters were filled, as my brother and I helped my Mom purge thirty years of accumulated stuff.

I know a licensed child care provider who runs a daycare out of her home. She is also a single mom of two pre-teens. One weekend, after listening to me preach about the "evils" of clutter, needing to move on with her life and stop hanging on to the past and watching Clean Sweep on TLC, she started clearing her paper clutter. This led to cleaning out and organizing all of the daycare toys. Over the past two months, at time of writing, she has emptied numerous Rubber Maid containers, had a huge rummage sale and is feeling more in control of her home and her stuff, and therefore her life. Going through and purging un-needed and un-used stuff is one of the most cathartic things you can do. She had found broken toys, hundreds of crayons/markers, games with missing pieces and lots of other "stuff" that was given to her by well-meaning friends and relatives, who cleared out THEIR stuff by giving it to her, under the guise of "it's for the day care." She felt GUILTY saying no to something free and for her business, yet her clutter had grown out of control and was taking over her life. She is now taking control of her home by saying NO to more stuff, trying to touch in-coming paper only once and teaching her kids to do likewise.

When de-cluttering toys, which is second only to paper clutter, it is imperative to keep age appropriateness in mind. If your child is now 4 years old, toys ages 1–2 years or even 2–4 years old should be put in the sell, donate or toss pile. But DeAnna, you say, I might have another child. Great, but are you pregnant now? Or, are you just "thinking" about having another child? How long do you intend to store and maintain tubs of toys and clothes? I have another friend who falls into this category. She and her husband have a 2 year-old girl. They MAY have another child, but not in the near future. This friend actually has tubs of clothes that are divided into categories: girl clothes- and then sub-divided by age, and then unisex clothes- and again divided by age (in case they have boy when and if they have another child.) All of these tubs are kept neatly stacked in her basement. Imagine all of the time and effort that went into this endeavor for something that may or may not happen. When and if it does, will the clothes be in style or even wearable? Do you see yourself in my friend?

Donate the clothes and toys to a worthy children's organization. There are children who could use these items right now. Think of the time and effort you are putting into maintaining items for an event that may not even occur. Items that you can keep would be "special" clothes that you can archive, the crib or rocker or some meaningful toys. Again, think of what truly has meaning. Go through the same process for toys and kids items that you do with your own things. Ask WHY the item is important. Is it your child's christening gown or the outfit you brought him/her home from the hospital in? Was the crib made by your father or painted by you and your spouse as you put together the nursery? In looking at what toys to keep, think about how your child has interacted with that toy. We all have our one special toy. Mine was my Mrs. Beasley doll. Your child will let you know.

Let's talk now about clothes clutter. We all have it. We have thin clothes, fat clothes, sloppy clothes, dress-up clothes, painting clothes…Ahhhhhh. Let me say this, if you still have clothes from over 10 years ago-unless it's a Prada suit-re-evaluate your wardrobe! If you are at a high school or college reunion and while looking through photos you recognize your CURRENT wardrobe, enlist some friends for an intervention at the mall. Your wardrobe should reflect the person you are now or would like to be. Think about dressing like the boss for that promotion! If your wardrobe looks like a throwback to your high school glory days or only represents one facet of your life (i.e. only suits-but no jeans, or only athletic shoes and sweats-but no dress clothes,) you need to carefully evaluate your clothes and see what they may say about your current life situation. Do you like what your wardrobe says about you?

From a feng shui stand point, if your wardrobe is unbalanced-only representing one or two life areas-look at what's missing. Is it an area you want to improve upon or work on? A friend was evaluating her wardrobe and getting ready to purge items when she realized that she had no "date" clothes. This came as quite a shock. Nothing was found that could even come close to being described as sexy. What is interesting about this is that this person was working on her Relationship area and really was trying to make an effort to improve this part of her life. Needless to say, that next weekend she grabbed one of her most objective friends and went to the mall. While her soul mate, at time of writing, has not been found yet, her confidence and focused attention on this area has improved, bringing about more opportunities in this life area. Again, look at your wardrobe and see what it is reflecting about your life. Do you like it? If not, change it.

It can't be stated enough that if you don't have positive feelings and/or use your "stuff," you shouldn't have it. You need to EMPTY out drawers, closets, shelves, containers...you get the idea. It's OK to give yourself permission to let things go and then DO IT. If you still can't bear the thought of parting with the bread machine "you had to have" for your birthday five years ago, put it in a box (along with any other items you just can't imagine your life without-but don't use) attach an index card stating what's inside and store it. You can store the container in the garage, basement, attic, empty closet or in an extra bedroom. Revisit "the box" in six months. If you haven't even thought about the contents and/or forgot the box even existed, you can comfortably take the entire box to Goodwill with a clear conscience.

Once you start on your "purge," you will be amazed at how much you really part with. If you are like my Mom, you will even start looking for more things to get rid of once you are finished. I still go through my closets and am amazed at some of the clothes that have escaped previous purges. I just took another bag to Goodwill this afternoon! I've started looking at the items I'm getting rid of and considering what I could have done with that money instead (a weekend in NYC, a month worth of Starbucks...you get the idea.)

In summary:

- If you don't love it, use it or need it-Get RID of it!
- If your child has outgrown items (toys, clothes...)-Get RID of them!
- If an item is broken, and you haven't fixed it, replaced it, or missed it-Get RID of it!
- If your clothes, collections, books...don't say who you are right now or where you want to be-Get RID of them!
- Give yourself permission to let go of items that you are hanging onto due to guilt or fear.
- Love what you have. You should enjoy your "stuff" not be stressed out by it.
- Use your stuff. Don't save things for "that special occasion." Everyday is special and should be treated as such. Make up a holiday if you have to, think of Mr. Costanza on Seinfeld with his Festivus for the rest of us!

What you will gain will far outweigh what you will lose. A sense of clarity and a sense of control over your space will wash over you, as you can now actually see your space and you living in it! You should own your stuff-it doesn't (or shouldn't) own you!

5

Utilize the Power Position

Create a focal point. Use a bright piece of artwork to draw your eye into the room. Use the fireplace, use the TV, and use the view...AHHHHHH! We all know we need to create a major "grouping" or area that sets the tone/theme of a room, but HOW do we know what to use, WHY do we need to do this and WHERE should it be located. The answers to these questions will be discussed in this section.

But wait, you say, what exactly is a focal point and how do I find it? A focal point is the spot where your eye immediately travels upon entering a space. When I was designing retail spaces, the focal point/area, was where we displayed our "featured" merchandise for the week, any seasonal items or anything that was featured in an ad or PR campaign. In a home setting, think of what says "you" or what sets the tone of the room. To find out where to place furniture or featured items (i.e. the room's focal point,) stand in the doorway of the space looking into the room and find the corner that is diagonal to the entryway. This is the Power Position of the space and where you want to create your focal point.

The WHY of creating a focal point is simple: a focal point gives the room a sense of purpose and helps determine the color scheme. In terms of seating, the focal point, or power position of the room, is also the most psychologically secure position in the space. It is your starting point in any (re) design of the room. A focal point can be created using the room's major furniture piece (desk, sofa...) a highlighted piece of artwork or an architectural feature. When I work with a client, we discuss how the room will be used, who will be using it and what HAS TO come back into the space. (In some cases, if an item doesn't work, I try to re-work the piece into another space.) Once that is determined, I start with how the room will be used. When looking at a bedroom, the bed is obviously going to be the focal point. If the room is an office, it's the desk. These pieces are what "set the theme" of the room. Sarah Susanka states in her book, *Home by Design*, that "a point of focus draws people in and adds character to a room…An unfocused room can be as disconcerting as a blurry photograph: your eye doesn't know where to look."

When the room isn't "easy to pin down" or is a multi-use room (i.e. a media room, family room, great room…) it's easier to pick out an architectural feature or some favorite piece of art/collectible. An architectural feature is easier to work with, rather than cover up. A fireplace, a built-in buffet/shelving or bay window are examples of architectural features that can be highlighted. However, when using an architectural feature as your focal point, you have no choice as to position and must work with where it currently exists. As luck would have it, most fireplaces are placed in the power position, or at least that quadrant, drawing you into the space. When the architectural feature isn't placed in the perfect spot, proper utilization of mirrors and seating space planning can help.

Lighting can also be used to create a focal point. If you haven't been to a lighting showroom, or even the lighting department at your local Home Depot or Lowe's…GO. This form of design has truly come into its own recently, and I even feel it's a form of art. Track lighting isn't the stick straight, ugly black track lighting from the 70s. It's now available in different colors, different mediums, a variety of bulbs (halogen or fluorescent, spot or flood) and shapes. You can truly configure the light where you need it and highlight what you want to emphasize. You can even put on dimmers or different switches to create "ambience" for whatever the occasion. However, if you still don't want to go the track lighting route, you can use a variety of ceiling mount chandeliers, ceiling fans…the list goes on. (I'm a fan of putting chandeliers wherever I can! I've even put them in bathrooms and bedrooms.) When doing any form of remodel or re-design, check in with a lighting designer, as your decision can totally change the atmosphere of your room.

When discussing the power position, you also need to consider placement of the main seating pieces. It is imperative that when seated, the head of the household should never have his/her back to the entryway of the space. Having your back to the door subconsciously keeps you on edge or "looking behind you." The room can also look uninviting to those entering the space, as the first thing they see is the back of people and furniture. This is especially useful in office settings. If an office is properly set-up, the occupant of the space should have the desk placed so that when seated at the desk, the occupant has a clear view of the doorway and whoever enters.

The power position is also a concern in the bedroom with placement of the bed. In terms of interior design, this is the most psychologically secure position in the room, which can help to secure a good night's sleep. The bed is also usually the largest piece of furniture in the room, and is often like a piece of art when you consider the amount of time and money spent on bedding. Therefore, placing it in the power position makes sense as it then becomes the room's focal point.

A lot has been written about the "Death Position" of bed placement and the relationship to feng shui. The Death Position occurs when the bed is placed IN DIRECT LINE with the doorway resulting in the feet pointing out of the door when the occupant is sleeping. This position derived its name from the custom of carrying a dead body out of a room feet first. Therefore, when you sleep in this position, you are imitating a corpse (pleasant thought, hey?) But DeAnna, you say, there is no other place for me to put the bed, how do I counteract this? Well, there a few ways to alleviate the problem:

- You can use fabric to create a canopy over the bed. The fabric becomes a "wall" with the bed then sitting in a niche. This also creates a cocoon of sorts and gives the feeling of security.
- Place a faceted crystal between the bed and door.
- Place a folding screen at the foot of the bed (See first tip.)

As I was recently walking into a friend's guest room, I glanced into her 10 year old daughter's room. Her bed was placed in the Death Position. I was so bothered by this; I made her change the space plan of the room immediately. (Yes, my friends LOVE having me visit.)

When you make use and highlight focal points in a space and arrange furniture groupings utilizing the power position, you create a welcoming environment to those who enter-a space that invites conversation and connection among the occupants and guests.

6

Utilize the 5 Senses in Your Décor/Design

Ahhhh the smell of fresh mowed grass…. The sound of birds chirping…The feel of a soft cashmere throw…. The sound of your neighbor's garage band "practicing" until 2am every night….

The sights and sounds around us affect our wellbeing, both consciously and subconsciously. We've all had noisy neighbors that have affected our sleep that in turn has affected our ability to perform at our best at work the next day. How about the neighbors in the next apartment who "think" they are gourmet cooks, much to the contrary smells coming from their apartment. Then there's the "artistic neighbor" who painted his house purple with polka dots "as a statement." (This is a true story from one of my old neighborhoods!) I'm sure his neighbors think of their property values every time they look out their windows!

Our environment is a major factor in how we interact with others as well as our mental and physical wellbeing. The goal of interior design is to create a space that is not only aesthetically pleasing, but also takes into consideration all of the activities that are to occur in the space (sleeping, cooking, entertaining, meeting clients…) Feng shui takes design one step further. Instead of working against your surroundings and trying to change them, you are working with and enhancing your environment. One of the ways you can bring this ancient art into your home, besides de-cluttering, is to try and get more "in tune" with your environment. I don't mean in a minimalist, no TV way (although if that's your idea of heaven, go for it.) By utilizing all of your senses you can create an environment that is balanced and more interesting, one that engages you with your surroundings.

OK-let's go through the five senses and how you can go about "engaging" them to create your environment. The five senses are: sight, sound, smell, touch and taste. The easiest sense to start with in design is sight. We see our furniture. We see the view out of our kitchen window. We see our artwork. We see the clutter gathering in the mudroom. (I told you clutter would be a theme discussed throughout.) This is also the easiest to fix. Let's go back to the lessons learned in the clutter chapter. If you don't have a positive association with an item, GET RID OF IT. Why do you want to look at something that makes you sad or angry? But DeAnna, you say, I have "no taste," "am color blind" or "don't know an Eames from a Chippendale".... There is hope. As much as I'd love to say, "you must have a designer" to help you with your home, I won't, because you have the power to create a space that is fit for you and your family. You know what you like. However, if you really are colorblind, I would suggest getting some help.

Look at your artwork and collections and see what the "theme" is. Meaning, do you have a collection of guns displayed or a collection of cat figurines. One has violent connotations, while the other has a more passive connotation. We can take it one step further to see what kind of cats is being displayed: domestic cats or tigers. See the difference? OK-you say to yourself, but I'm a hunter and I "have a positive association with the guns." That may be, but on the whole, guns have a violent association for most people.

Where the items are being displayed is also important. You may like your gun collection, but you wouldn't, and shouldn't, display them in your bedroom. Rather, it's more likely that the collection would be perfectly placed in your den. In feng shui, you must also look at what a room's purpose is. The bedroom reflects romance/rest. The family room is for social/entertaining/family gatherings. Your artwork, collections and colors should enhance the purpose of the room. In speaking of artwork and collections, make sure that these items are inspiring and meaningful. Otherwise, the space can look unbalanced, uninviting and blah. Remove any images that are hung up only to cover up a bare wall.

Color has meaning? You bet it does. There are cool and warm colors. Cool colors are: blues, purples, blue/greens, and some whites. Warm colors are: reds, oranges, yellows, yellow/greens and some whites. Now, when speaking about color, remember that there are hundreds of colors in a variety of tints (color with white added,) shades (color with black added) and tones. Warm colors tend to excite and have been shown to raise our blood pressure. Use a warm color when you want to encourage activity. Think of the color schemes of fast food restaurants: red/orange/yellow: food eaten fast. Cool colors should be used when you want to rest or meditate. I always use cool colors in bedrooms to promote a better night's sleep. Now, that being said, I'm not saying you can NEVER use a warm color in a bedroom or a cool color in a family room. I am saying you shouldn't use them as the primary color but rather as an accent. Again, remember the psychology of the color and the activity of the room and match them.

Still confused on color? Here are some of the meanings for primary and secondary colors:

RED-the most physical color, raises blood pressure, creates a sense of urgency, danger, excitement, vitality, ambition, anger. Too much red can cause irritation, impatience and anger. **PINK** is a gentler version of red and is soothing and calming, alleviates oversensitivity and surrounds us with a sense of love and protection. Research is being done on using this color in prisons to lessen violent tendencies of prisoners.

ORANGE-the color most linked with creativity, drama, happiness, and a wonderful anti-depressant. It is also the most uncomfortable color for most people. Orange is related to the digestive tract and increasing its function. For this reason, do not use it in your kitchen if weight is an issue, or if you are on a diet. **PEACH** is a gentler version and good for nervous exhaustion.

YELLOW-alertness, clear-headed, decisive, color of the sun. It is also one of the hardest colors for the brain to "break down." When using this color, make sure it's a clear and not dull yellow. Yellow is related physically with the nervous system-it excites. Use yellow sparingly if any of the inhabitants of the space exhibit any mental illnesses such as ADD, ADHD or hyperactivity. Never use yellow in a child's bedroom, rather, use earth tones. Yellow should be used primarily as an accent color. It is great for use in an office or any other room where mental functions/study are the primary activity.

GREEN-nature's color, the most balancing of the colors, related with the heart and regulating circulation, growth, new beginnings, comfort in times of stress. It is frequently the color choice in hospitals and is a perfect color in any room. Use yellow-greens sparingly as it is hard on the eye. In general, any green found in nature can be used as a neutral.

BLUE-the most popular color, soothing, cooling, calming, lowers blood pressure, anti-inflammatory. Deep blue stimulates the pituitary gland, which helps to regulate deep sleep. It is the perfect color for bedrooms. Blue should not be used in a kitchen as it "grays out" the food and makes it unappetizing. However, if you are trying to lose weight, eat on a blue plate! Too much blue, especially dark blue can be depressing.

TURQUOISE-refreshing, calming as it combines blue and green. Think of the waters off the Caribbean...Ahhhhhhhhhhhh. It is invigorating, cooling and great when under mental strain. It is good for studios, studies, bedrooms, and bathrooms.

INDIGO/PURPLE/VIOLET-cooling, suppresses hunger, spiritual, peace, artistic endeavors. A great color for bedrooms, meditation rooms or any other room where quiet is emphasized.

WHITE-ultimate purity, peace, protection, cleansing, freedom. Too much can be cold and isolating. Use it in combination with any color. White is perfect in kitchens and bathrooms where cleanliness is key!

BLACK-protective, mysterious, associated with silence, passive. Too much black can be depressing, oppressive and indicate "hiding" from the world. Use as an accent with any color.

GRAY-independent, self-reliant, authoritative. Too much conotates fog, smoke, evasion and non-commitment (neither black nor white.) Use as an accent color in an office or a teenager's room.

SILVER-emotional, sensitive, balancing, mentally cleansing. It is a great accent in a bedroom or bathroom.

GOLD-sunny, abundance, power, wisdom, understanding, energizing, inspiring. Gold is a perfect accent in an office, family room or kitchen.

BROWN/EARTH TONES-color of Mother Earth, stable, is grounding, solid. Too much is boring and denotes an inability to move forward. Earth tones can be used as an accent with any color in any room.

If you want to learn more about color and how it affects our lives and how you can use it in other aspects of your life, check out the book *The Complete Book of Color* by Suzy Chiazzari. This is my color bible. I strongly recommend it.

OK-now on to smell. We all know what smells good to us: fresh mowed grass; chocolate chip cookies baking in the oven; fresh flowers…. We also know what smells are repulsive to us: a wet dog, burned food, garbage sitting out on a hot day…Our sense of smell is so strong and ingrained in our psyche that a hint of certain smells can transport us back years in our memory banks to a place and time in our past-good or bad. Smell a rose and you're immediately transported back to being with your grandfather as he tended his rose garden. You get the picture. Our olfactory system is as important to design as our sense of sight. How can you enjoy that beautiful new bedroom and get a good night's sleep, if all you can smell is that fake lavender scented candle next to your bed?

Historically, perfume was first intended for use in "changing our surroundings" not for scenting our bodies. Ancient cultures, from the Greeks and Romans to the Chinese, relied on burning various plants to enhance their environment, and influence and alter their bodies and minds in a therapeutic way. Now, with the home-fragrance industry topping $1.4 billion a year, we are now being sold on "environmental fragrancing" as scents are being used everywhere from our home and car to restaurants and stores.

Dr. Alan Hirsch, a neurologist and psychiatrist who headed up the Smell and Taste Treatment and Research Foundation in Chicago, has done many studies that show that scent can be an important addition to our environment when used to complement architecture or to make it friendlier. For example, green apple or cucumber, tend to make tight areas seem larger, while BBQ smoke makes a room feel smaller. Hirsch states that a "mixed floral scent can enhance learning ability." Use peppermint in the kitchen if you're trying to lose weight, or use lavender or vanilla in the bedroom to help you sleep at night.

Hirsch goes on to say that "the way your home smells is interpreted as the way you are." Meaning, if your home smells good, you and your home are viewed positively, or vice versa. You adapt to odors you are exposed to after only 10–20 minutes. That's why people who smoke are immune to the smell of smoke on themselves. However, if you don't smoke, you notice the smell immediately. When trying to evaluate your home and its smells, bring in a 3rd party to help you discertain anything amiss. Find the cause and fix it (i.e. mold/mustiness from too much humidity.)

Since smell is tied to memory, surround yourself with scents that bring you back to times and places you enjoyed. I cannot emphasize enough that healthy, natural choices are imperative here. Many people are affected with environmental sensitivities, and the mere whiff of a synthetic perfume can send them grabbing their inhalers. So, if you or any family member are bothered by allergies, asthma or have any other propensity to upper respiratory disorders, migraines and even fatigue-Go Natural! People also tend to respond to scent better if it is accompanied by a visual (i.e. pinecones displayed with pine scent in room,) hence potpourri's widespread use.

You can add scent to your space in a variety of ways:

- Add candles-look for soy, palm or beeswax with cotton wicks to avoid the smoking and sooting that can occur.
- Use room sprays.
- Burn incense.
- Utilize fragrance wax or oil burners.
- Add potpourri (also plays into sight.)
- Place light bulb rings on lights and use room diffusers.
- Use perfumed pillows and sachets.

When choosing a scent, always take into account the activity of the room. You don't want to use lavender in a kitchen or peppermint in a bedroom. The scents of many plants have a psychological effect on us. All parts of plants and flowers are used and can be dried or harvested for their essential oils. When purchasing essential oils, or any of the above-mentioned items, look for natural ingredients and stay away from things labeled "fragrance" as these are man-made and use synthetic ingredients. These are usually petroleum based and can cause adverse reactions in people who have allergies, asthma, are prone to migraines/headaches or the elderly or very young.

Utilize these scents to enhance the environment of any room.

- Bergamot-clean, citrus/floral scent thought to be regenerating

- Grapefruit-clean, citrus scent thought to help balance appetite, lift the spirits and quell mood swings
- Green apple-fruity scent can reduce anxiety and claustrophobia
- Jasmine-a sweet floral scent believed to be an antidepressant, a tranquilizer
- Lavender-a floral/herbal scent that has been found to be relaxing, soothing, rejuvenating, deodorizing and anti-bacterial, believed to enhance the immune system and alleviate depression
- Lemon-a sunny, citrus scent found to be antiseptic and rejuvenating
- Orange-a tangy citrus scent thought to be uplifting and balancing
- Peppermint-a fresh scent found to be rejuvenating, antiseptic and cleaning
- Rose-a floral scent believed to be an antidepressant, an aphrodisiac, a sedative and an antiseptic
- Rosemary-a spicy scent found to be antiseptic, regulating, astringent and cerebrally stimulating
- Sandalwood-a nutty, woody scent believed to be antiseptic, antidepressant and aphrodisiacal
- Vanilla-a sweet orchid scent proven to be relaxing and reassuring, and the #1 favorite scent of men.

Now let's examine the sense of touch. We all know how a luxurious cashmere throw feels on a cold winter day as opposed to a cotton sheet. How about the difference between an Italian leather sofa as opposed to one made of a nylon/polyester blend? I'm not trying to make the point that one texture is better than the other, but rather the difference and "feeling" you get when you touch and experience these things. Touch plays a big part in design and in creating the right "feel" of a space. You wouldn't use burlap in a bedroom, and you shouldn't use carpet in a bathroom. Burlap is not a soft, sensuous fabric that you would think of for comfort in falling asleep, but you could use a coarse texture in the bedroom as an accessory. In design, texture is used to create more VISUAL interest (there's sight again,) create a more interactive experience and exciting space. Think of a child's playroom or schools that have walls with different textures to help kids learn.

The easiest way to do this is by adding accent pillows in a variety of materials to a sofa or on the floor, or a luxurious throw on the back of a chair. How about the bowls of balls, pinecones or marbles that proliferate every home décor store? All of these accessories add interest to any space.

The next of the five senses is the sense of hearing. A bad view you can hide with curtains, a bad smell can be eradicated once the source is found, for touch you can add a pillow...but a bad sound? You bet. The barking dog next door, the teenager down the block who insists his/her car stereo is stuck on 60, the neighbor who MUST mow his lawn at 6am...we've all had experiences with bad sound. Unless you have a mature relationship with your neighbors and can work out a compromise, or you move, your options to control sounds external to your residence are limited. Sound proofing your home with landscaping, heavy drapes, more insulation and wall-coverings can help. (Cork on the walls of your child's room can deaden the sound of their stereo-it also serves as a BIG bulletin board.)

You can more easily control the sounds within your space. The right choice in wall and window coverings can create a cocoon in a bedroom. A tiled floor and walls in a bathroom create a cavernous, echo effect. Add fluffy towels, a thick bath mat and some plants. Music, wind chimes, pets (think of an aquarium and the hum of the filter, or your own barking dog,) the TV or tabletop fountain all help to create atmosphere in your space. Sound is very personal. What is relaxing and comforting to one can be irritating to another. I personally think the sound of trains is pleasant, as it brings back fond memories of past adventures, while others may find it jarring. When adding to or taking away sound from any space, check with other occupants and take their likes and dislikes into consideration when making the decision.

Here are some ways to control the volume in your space:

1.   Make your home a haven of tranquility. To absorb sound, place rubber feet under major appliances, and foam pads under small appliances. Area rugs and drapes will also help to control and absorb sound.

2.   Tune out the outside world. Concentrate on a pleasant view, daydream or put on headphones to "blot out" an unpleasant sound.

3.   Give your brain a break. Play a white noise machine or play a blank tape or CD to tune out airplane, train or "neighborhood" noise. By doing this, you are turning your attention inward, and your mind can stop racing and worrying.

The last of the five senses is taste. Although not commonly thought of in terms of design, good foods not only make us feel better, but can contribute to an overall more pleasing environment. While you can't have tasty treats in every room, although it has been suggested a bowl of M&Ms in each room would be a positive, you can make what is incorporated in the appropriate spaces good. Always buy the best quality food and ingredients you can afford. This gives the sense and feeling of abundance.

Remember the scene in "It's a Wonderful Life" when Mary Bailey is greeting the Martini's at their new home in Bailey Park? She greets them with bread "so they may never know hunger." I'm not saying you need to keep a fully stocked pantry, especially if you live alone and don't cook, that's just wasteful. However, keeping some supplies on hand that you use and enjoy will help create a space that is filled with positive energy. Another example is having a pitcher of water on your nightstand, so that if you get thirsty in the middle of the night, water is on hand.

Let's examine how effectively using the five senses can improve our attitude, our personal space and ultimately our life. When incorporating all five senses in your bedroom, you'd start with sight. Pick out the proper color that is pleasant to all occupants of the space, as well as, fitting for the bedroom. Once the color scheme is picked, you'd pick out the bedding and furniture. The furniture should fit the space and not be too big. Artwork should be romantic or calming in nature (not any battle scenes please!) Bedding is the perfect place to add texture (touch) in high thread count sheets, blanket, comforter and pillows. When adding sound, think soft, classical music to set whatever mood you are trying to create. If you just want a good night's sleep, refer to the sound blocking ideas. Smell? Add a bowl of lavender or ylang ylang to promote a good night's sleep or romance. At the very least, make sure bedding is fresh smelling. Taste can be accomplished with a pitcher of water at bedside to prevent the late night visit to the kitchen for something to drink. In conclusion, when utilizing the five senses in your home and in each room, you create a balanced space and a space that engages you as you interact within your surroundings.

7

Utilize the 5 Elements in Your Space's Décor/Design

In your quest to create a balanced space and lifestyle, and by keeping in mind the 9 Life Areas of the Bagua board, adding the five elements to your space is an easy way to add excitement and really change the energy of a room. Plus, by prioritizing and focusing on which of the life areas you want to activate, the addition of the required element will help in achieving your goals. (Refer to the chart in Chapter 2.)

The five elements are water, fire, metal, earth and wood. Some schools of thought will say air should also be included. I have been taught, however, that the energy we are trying to change is the air. You can add an element by adding an item made of the actual elemental material, or by the shape or color that represents its characteristics. Confusing, I know, but we'll try and make sense of it.

WOOD is an easy element to visualize. It includes furniture, plants, and figurines. Pictures of trees and forest landscapes are also representative of the wood element. Most of us can look around our rooms now and see at least one item that represents the wood element. Wood is also represented by the color green and by the shape of the rectangle.
EX: healthy green, upward growing plant

The element of **FIRE** can be represented with candles or fireplaces. Both are great examples of fire. The sun and stars, pictures of famous people or people you admire, the stove and pyramids are also fire related objects. Fire is represented by the color red, and its derivatives, and by the triangle.
EX: a red candle

The element of **METAL** is usually seen in appliances, bath/kitchen fixtures or light fixtures. Metal can also be found in various accessories such as candleholders, sculptures, picture frames and coins. The color white and all metallics are associated with the metal element and by the shape of a circle.
EX: a handful of coins

WATER is one of the more popular elements you will find in peoples' décor and is second only to wood. Water is seen in water-related pictures (ocean, lake, river, waterfall scenes,) water-related animals (dolphins, frogs,) tabletop fountains, free-flowing fabrics (such as swags on curtains) and mirrors. The colors blue and black, and free-flowing lines represent water, as water is mutable and can take on the shape of the container it is held in.

The **EARTH** element is the hardest one for people to visualize and implement in their home. Any item made from the earth: clay, brick, stone, marble/granite and tile. If you have ceramic tile in your home, you have earth represented. Do you have a terra cotta holder for a plant? You have Earth. Earth is represented by color in all earth tones and yellow. The shape is a square.

OK-let's examine how this can work in a home. The easiest room to start with is the bathroom. Most already have at least 3 or 4 of the elements already! Here goes. In a bathroom, you have either tile on the floor, the walls or perhaps in the shower-Earth. Ceramic or vinyl floor tile is also usually square-Earth. The bathroom is a water room with a tub, sink and toilet. In addition most people do water themes as part of the bathroom decoration. I would discourage this, as it becomes an overabundance of water. Refer to the chapter on bathrooms for more on this topic. The fixtures on the sink, tub and shower represent metal. Your vanity and cabinetry are typically made of wood. Plants are also commonly found in the bathroom adding more wood. Your bathmats and towels are typically rectangle as well...wood again. Fire is the element that is usually missing and can be brought in by adding candles and/or red/pink/burgundy to the color scheme.

But DeAnna, I don't like/am afraid of color...how can I do this? Here's an example of how you can add the five elements without using color. Assuming a monochromatic room with a tan carpet and white walls. Let's do a family room given this color constraint. First, it will have wood furniture including a rectangular cocktail and side tables. A fireplace will have metal accessories for cleaning. If there isn't a fireplace, how about some red candles in metal/iron holders to add fire. For water, a tabletop fountain is ideal. If you don't want that sound, pictures of water scenes, in wood or metal frames, will do the trick. Earth is represented by the brick on the above-mentioned fireplace or by terra cotta pots for plants. Square area rugs will also help to bring earth into the room. Mission accomplished: a well-balanced room in a neutral color scheme.

8

Bring the Outdoors In-
Welcoming in Mother Nature

We all know that there is a type of inner healing that we experience from being outside in all of Mother Nature's glory for even an hour or two. Being amongst the trees, flowers and even digging in the dirt can make the worst day fade into a distant memory. When I say enjoy nature, it can be a challenge for those of us who live in the northern climates, as mid-January is not very hospitable for gardening. However, even getting outside for a few minutes, like taking the dogs out for a brisk walk around the block can make a difference. But how do you get the benefits of Mother Nature inside your home without freezing, literally, or rolling around in the mud (figuratively?) Simple, you can bring some of the outside in.

Today, our society is so insulated from nature, with our homes being closed off from the slightest draft and county parks and other green spaces declining in our urban areas. You don't even have to go outside to get in your car or from your car to your place of business, thanks to attached garages and parking structures! During winter hours, there are times when you can go a whole day without knowing if the sun is out. That's sad. Studies have shown you need to get outside for at least 15 minutes a day to produce melatonin, which helps regulate your system and sleep cycles. It also helps to air out "your brain" when working on a tough problem or when you're having "a day."

Bringing green plants into your space is the single easiest way to bring nature inside. Having plants in your home can accomplish many things. Plants help to detoxify the air you breathe improving air quality. One plant for every 100 square feet of space is recommended for optimal benefits. A later chapter deals with specific plants to bring into your space for subsequent health benefits. Plants also bring in the wood element, which has been previously discussed. It is needed to help balance the space and, in feng shui terms, promote "growth and new beginnings."

From a feng shui perspective, plants bring in a needed life force and energy to any space they occupy. That being said, make sure that when you do bring plants into your space, you maintain them. Trim any dead leaves and "dead head" the plant when a bloom is done flowering. Dead plants suck the energy force out of a room, besides adding clutter and negative vibes to the space. Dried plants also fall into the "dead plant" category. Dried wreaths and bundles should be disposed of. If you are like my Mom, however, and can't part with EXPENSIVE wreaths you purchased (again refer to Clutter chapter) make sure that the wreaths are in life areas that you aren't working on or needs improvement. Examples of this would be the RELATIONSHIP area at all times (unless you are a hermit) or the WEALTH/ABUNDANCE area if your finances are a concern.

***Remember to get upward growing plants, as you want to draw your eye, and energy, upward!* **

Plants are also the epitome of nature-it's what people think of when they say nature. The great thing about bringing plants into the home is that you can find plants that require little care and light, or, if you really are into gardening, plants that you "can baby." Go to any garden center, flower shop, grocery store or home improvement store, and you can find plants in any size, shape and price range.

***Live in an apartment? Try growing herbs in a kitchen window! They don't take up a lot of space, are easy to care for, smell good and can be used for cooking, if you are so inclined.* **

OK-so you don't have a green thumb, but enjoy nature and want to reap its benefits anyway; what are you to do? How about incorporating nature-related accessories in your décor? This can be a seashell, a dish of pebbles/rocks you gathered on a hike or a bowl of sand that can be used for holding lighted votives. People have even made lamps out of antlers! For the truly crafty, twigs can be an addition on picture frames or candleholders. Stone, wood, tile and brick are also natural materials that give you that outdoor feel. These natural elements add color and texture to any organic design.

Choosing patterns and colors that reflect the outdoors are also ways to bring nature into your space. Rustic terra cottas, browns, leafy greens and cool blues are all natural colors. If you see it in nature, it goes, and remember, green is a neutral in nature. Leaf patterns, florals and water inspired abstracts are prints that can be used in drapes, rugs, pillows, throws and upholstery patterns to reflect outdoor scenes.

Today, rugs and wall coverings are being made from a variety of natural materials. Bamboo, grass cloth, sisal, jute and coconut fibers are all available. These fibers are durable, fairly easy to maintain, competitively priced and bring the nature element into any space in which they are used.

Artwork, photos and figurines made out of natural materials and depicting nature scenes can also help to bring nature to your indoor space. Artwork can include paintings, limited edition prints or sketches. These and photos of wildlife and outdoor scenes are popular no matter what your geographic area is. Nature-related pictures are also great souvenirs to remind you of a great trip and can be used to transport you back to that special place and time. Examples: beach/shoreline, forest/woods, prairies, mountains and/or an animal found in the wild. This type of artwork is applicable for men or women and as a result, graces many a family room and even master bedroom.

Here are some "green thoughts" about our newly designed life and home and why it's important to bring the outside in:

1. Living in tune with nature is an invitation to live creativity. Just look at Mother Nature as your "creativity teacher." No two days; no two snowflakes; and no two clouds are the same.

2. Nourish your soul; eat the freshest, most natural foods you can find.

3. The earth is alive. It breathes, grows and evolves.

4. Enjoy an unplugged activity every day. Don't rely on your Playstation to complete you!

5. Think of nature as a destination in itself, not something to just drive through.

6. Your home is part of the environment. Keep it pollution free.

7. Change doesn't happen with a single action, but with a series of small gestures.

You don't have to make the inside of your home look like a garden or a forest, but bringing in some of the elements that are nature-related will help you to de-stress and help to create a mini-personal sanctuary in a crazy world.

9

Maintaining a Welcome and Unobstructed Entryway

You walk in the door after a hard day out in the world. You throw your keys somewhere on a table. Your coat gets "hung" over the closest chair. Your shoes get kicked off somewhere across the floor and your briefcase, bags and backpacks get dumped on the nearest flat surface. Does this sound familiar? This same scenario plays out in homes everywhere, whether you walk through the front door, the back door, the garage or the mudroom. However that doesn't make it right.

In feng shui terms, the foyer or front entryway is the space that acts as a transition between the stress of the outside world and your "inner sanctum." It is also the gateway through which positive energy enters your home. It is important that you use your front door on a daily basis. But DeAnna, you say, I drive into the garage and enter the house through the garage door (or through the back door if you have an unattached garage)...Am I doomed? No. I also, enter through the back door of my house; however, I always use the front door to get my mail, water outside plants or to walk my dogs. Even if you just open the door and walk through it, you are still "activating" good, welcoming energy and bringing it into your space. (Your neighbors might think you're a little off kilter, but what the heck.)

When evaluating your foyer or front entrance, here are some key things to look at:

- Is it well lit?
- Are the address numbers clearly labeled?
- What is the status of the landscaping? Are there empty flowerpots or worse yet, dead plants inside? Are the trees and bushes overgrown?

- Is the front porch cluttered with toys, furniture or other "outside" decorations?
- Does the doorway open freely into your home?
- Can you step into and throughout the space without having to step over things?
- Is there a stairway that begins/ends at the front door?
- Is there a wall right as you walk in subconsciously stopping you from entering?
- Is the space inviting? Do you want to go any further into the space?

Most of these are easy to fix, once you realize the effect they have on you, your guests and your space. Stand on the walk, or drive, looking at your home. This is something that must be done if you are thinking of selling your home. Really take the time and look at it impartially. What do you see? Do you see a neatly kept lawn and yard or trees so overgrown they tower over the house? An afternoon in the sun with a trimmer will do your yard and you good. Can you navigate the walk leading up to house or are you tripping over bikes? If you can't make it to the house in one piece, how can your guests (or good energy?) Remove the blocks! Upon reaching the door, are the address numbers easy to read? Is there a doorbell or knocker to announce your arrival? What is the state of the front door and trim? Is there peeling paint? These are all afternoon or weekend projects that will do wonders for the look and appeal of your home. As a result, it will attract more attention and, from a feng shui standpoint, more opportunity.

Upon entering the space, you should be able to fully open the door to allow energy, and people in. This is applicable to all doors in your space. If you can, get rid of the stuff behind the door THAT IS BLOCKING and hindering this activity. When standing inside the entryway, what do you see? Can you see? Most people don't have the proper wattage bulb in their light fixtures. This area needs to be clutter free for all to enter and exit easily. This area sets the tone for the rest of the space. What artwork, if any, is displayed here? Most people put a mirror here with a flower arrangement. My suggestion is to only utilize a mirror if there is something to reflect. Meaning, don't put a mirror up mistakenly thinking it will "enlarge the space." A mirror must reflect something. If the only purpose of your mirror is to reflect back the image of whoever is entering your room, take it down. That is jarring to the psyche and very unsettling. In feng shui terms, you are reflecting the energy entering your space right back out the door!

A stairway that begins and ends at the front door also causes problems. Stairways are conductors of energy, as are hallways. This particular location of stairs conducts energy right out the front door from the upper level. You want energy to "spend time" or meander throughout your home. Your goal is to slow this down. You can do this in a variety of ways. Any and all photos or artwork that are displayed on the stairway need to be detail oriented to bring people to the picture and curious to see more. The top of the stairs needs to be well-lit and "lighter" than the lower level, meaning a lighter paint color should be chosen to attract the eye, and energy, up. A funky light fixture can be placed here to really lift the eye upward. Chandeliers are also wonderful ways to light entryways. An interesting figurine or piece of furniture should be placed near the top of the stairs to, again, attract attention up.

*** *A quick feng shui cure is to place a crystal between the stairs and the doorway.* ***

Now that I have most of you in tears and ready to move, let me say, there is hope. First, work and fix the easy things. We discussed getting out and spending the afternoon working outside on the lawn and plants. If you don't have a green thumb and this just panics you to no end, minimize your landscaping. No one will think any worse of you if you don't have x amount of trees, border flowers and raised flower beds. Work within what makes you comfortable, and if that means having just a lawn with no landscaping, great, make it the best lawn you can. Home Depot and Lowe's make it very easy to update/fix the "door jewelry" such as kick plates, doorbells, mailboxes, locks and address numbers. I did this myself in an afternoon on a house I was selling at a cost under $200. What a difference! However, time and cost will change if you have to paint or change out doors. This cost can be re-cooped when you sell. Better yet, think of the pride you'll have as you continue to live there.

Feng shui also dictates that there is some sort of movement to attract positive energy and opportunity to the space. Now you get to utilize what I call the "car lot" approach. Picture yourself driving down the street. Your eye automatically goes to the movement of multi-colored flags waving in the wind, and then you see…the cars. So whether you are looking for a car or not, your eye is looking at the lot due to the movement of the flags. So, do you need to post lines of plastic flags throughout your property? No. Think in terms of wind chimes, garden flags, whirligigs, windsocks, fountains or weathervanes.

***A note to feng shui initiates: the material you use for wind chimes is dependent on the direction your house faces! A fountain or other feature should only be used if your home faces N, SE, W or NW. ***

Now that the outside looks fabulous, what about some ideas to improve the inside? A warm color scheme should be picked for this space. Use reds, yellows, oranges and greens. Plants at the front door and inside also help to create a welcoming, positive impression to your guests. Any artwork used here should be detail oriented, as on the stairs, to draw people into the space. That is your goal, right? I'm also a huge fan of area rugs at the entrance and runners to help anchor the space and help to direct traffic into the space. Think of runners as the pathways into and throughout your space. Runners can also be used if you have a half-wall that you "walk into" upon entering the foyer, as the rug will lead you away from the wall and into a larger area. If you still need to use a mirror, because you just can't part with it, put the mirror on a sidewall flanking the door, not on the wall directly opposite it. Then on the opposite wall have a plant or artwork so that is what is reflected back into the space.

These same rules apply to the mudroom or back door. Make the entry from the back as pretty as the front. Check out the condition of the door and locks. Do they work? Is the door secure? Make whatever improvements are necessary. From a feng shui and security standpoint, this area also needs to be well lit, especially if you arrive home at night!

The main difference between a front and back entrance is that the back entrance tends to see more traffic and is typically treated as a dumping ground. I suggest multi-use furniture here to accommodate the needs of boots, backpacks, dog leashes and keys. A trunk that doubles as a seat is great to hold scarves, gloves and hats, and you can then sit on it to put on your boots. If there is room, a baker's rack or something similar is great to organize all of your pet supplies from food to leashes, as well as sweaters and towels to wipe off muddy paws. Otherwise, hooks are a great alternative. Coats, scarves and backpacks can all be held and will keep items off of the floor and readily available.

***Flooring in both entryways should be a hard surface for easier maintenance. Hard surfaces are: tile, vinyl, marble or hardwood. These are high traffic areas and will need to be cleaned frequently…make it as low-maintenance as possible! ***

Another consideration for the entryway is to look at what rooms are visible from the front door. Remember, this is the first impression people get upon entering. Do they see a toilet through an open door to a powder room? Keep this door closed at all times. Do they see right into the kitchen? They, or you, will subconsciously be thinking of food and when you'll eat. Is a bedroom visible from the front door? The person who has this room to sleep in will suffer from restless sleep due to being in an "active" part of the home. Ideally you should be entering into a great room, media room or family room. A home office/den is also fine for the front part of the house, especially if you will be meeting clients there. You really don't want strangers tramping through your house to get to your office.

10

Addressing the Bathroom or Don't Flush Away Your Finances!

According to home remodelers, the kitchen and bathroom are where a majority of homeowner's spend their money when making home improvements. We add bathrooms, we increase the size of existing bathrooms, we change fixtures and cabinetry, and we add whirlpool tubs. But to what end? When you were looking for your new home, you looked for a large bathroom, and were POSITIVE you were going to use the whirlpool tub once a week. It's now been 2 years and have you used it yet? A lot of people think they need to make these changes to increase their home's value not because they want or will use the upgrades.

***Note-if you're planning on making any home improvements, make them for you and your family to enjoy, not speculating that it may make you money. Some improvements will allow you to recoup most, if not all of your expenses, but again, make improvements only when and if you have to, and then you can enjoy them. ***

One home improvement task to undertake immediately is to fix any plumbing problems that occur. A dripping faucet can mean money "dripping away." Clogged pipes can be related to health issues of the digestive tract. It should also be noted that a clogged pipe or leaky faucet are easy quick things to fix; a $2 washer for the faucet or some Drano to unblock a hair clog, are usually all you need. Fix the small problems BEFORE they become big ones, otherwise you really will see your money go down the drain as you pay the plumber!

The bathroom has received a lot of bad press in terms of feng shui. Because of its relationship to the element of Water, the state of your bathroom is also symbolic of your wealth. Therefore, it is imperative in feng shui terms, to keep this area clean, clutter-free and keep the energy moving in an upward motion. Now, this last one is difficult, since the whole purpose of the bathroom is to take things down and away…not where you want your money going! Also, the more money you spend on increasing the size of the bathroom and other desired accoutrements, the more money "goes down the drain."

So, how do you counter-act this? How do you keep the energy flowing upward and not downward? One of the first things you can do is close all drains. This doesn't mean you close the plunger, it simply means you place a drain cover on any uncovered drains (this also goes for the kitchen.) An uncovered drain is an open invitation for energy (and theoretically money) to disappear down the drain.

Next, and ladies this is for you, keep the toilet seat down. An open, uncovered toilet bowl is the same as an uncovered drain. So the next time you "almost hit the water" tell the men in the house that they are messing with the family's finances! In feng shui, the ideal position for the toilet is not in the bathroom at all, but in a separate room by itself. If your toilet is in the bathroom, place a wind chime between it and the entryway to distract the attention of the energy flowing through the room. The toilet is one of the strongest drains of beneficial energy in the home or business. Stand at the door of the bathroom. If the toilet is the first thing you see when you enter, place a flowering potted plant on the top of the toilet tank, or position a statue on the floor next to the toilet to draw your eye away from the energy-draining fixture. The plant will help to uplift and counter-act the downward flow of the water and energy, and the statue will help to ground and stabilize the space.

*****Always flush with the lid down so that money-associated with Water-is not symbolically flushed away. *****

Another quick tip is to keep the bathroom door closed. In ancient times, the bathroom wasn't in the house and certainly not as clean or hygienic as modern-day bathrooms are (or should be) now. Mirrors on the outside of bathroom doors can effectively hide the bathroom or "make it disappear" as the mirror will reflect the scene outside room.

OK-we've gone over some basic feng shui tips to keep energy in the bathroom up, but what can you do to keep it growing and moving upward? A well-lit room is key, both from a feng shui and a safety perspective. You want to see what you're doing right (i.e. applying make-up, fixing your hair, shaving.) Lighting in the bathroom should come from above (general) and from the sides, so there are no shadows on the face. For safety reasons, the shower should also have a light. This is code in many communities. The ceiling light should be bright and stylish to set the mood of the room. It is worth taking a trip to a Home Depot or Lowe's lighting department to see what is currently available. The choices are amazing. Just remember, you can't use track lighting in the bathroom! I've put chandeliers in bathrooms for a great and grand effect! Anything goes in a bathroom, so you can really think out of the box and have fun.

If you are lucky enough to have a window in your bathroom, you can also bring in more light and energy by placing sun catchers and crystals in the window. Maximize natural light whenever possible, and open that window when you can to bring in fresh air. Ventilation is vital in this room to keep humidity down and inhibit mold and mildew. If you don't have a fan currently installed, this home improvement is a must. Make sure you buy a fan that is the right size for your room's square footage. Any licensed electrician can install this for you.

I personally am not a wallpaper or border fan, however, a border in the bathroom is OK. Borders help to bring your eye, and energy, up as your eye automatically goes to color and pattern. The ceiling color should also be lighter than the wall color. You can install crown molding to add an element that would add beauty to the room and bring the eye up. It should also be noted that wallpaper and other wall coverings tend to stop the walls from "breathing" and can encourage mold build-up if moisture gets behind it. Most wallpaper is made of vinyl which off-gasses and can create respiratory problems. Just say "no" to wallpaper in this room.

All surfaces in the bathroom, as well as the kitchen, should be hard surfaces that will make the room easier to maintain. Hard surfaces are tile, wood, laminates and stone. Carpet should never be placed in here. Simple bath mats can be used to bring in color and can then be thrown in the washer. Hair, soap scum, high humidity...all make this room a disaster waiting to happen. Keep it as easy to clean as possible.

Although we will talk about healthy choices for cleaners and the like in a later chapter, it is worth mentioning the importance of natural cleaning products and bath and body products. The bathroom, as shown historically, is for purifying and cleansing, so after cleaning your body, why do you want to slap a bunch of chemicals and toxins on it? Why do you want to clean this "pure" space with toxins? With the rise in the previously mentioned environmental sensitivities and other maladies, manufacturers have responded with a variety of choices in products that meet our healthy standards. Seventh Generation is a leader in natural home cleaners, and their products can be found at most large grocery store chains. Tom's of Maine (toothpaste, deodorant, soap) is also readily available. You don't need to search out the far corners of your city to try and make a socially responsible and healthy choice for your home and family. A quick search on the Internet will also yield a plethora of choices for you.

If you're really ambitious, you can make your own cleaners. Some great books are *Green Clean* (my favorite,) *Natural Housekeeping* and *Allergy Free Living.*

Some helpful cleaning tips to keep your bathroom sparkling clean and healthy follow:

- To keep mold and mildew at bay on your shower curtain and liner, toss them in the washing machine with some towels and then hang on a line to dry. In regards to "having a shower curtain AND a liner," take a cue from hotels, says Danny Seo, host of *Simply Green* on Lime (Sirius Radio) and use only a 100% nylon curtain, which is watertight and needs no liner. If you go the natural fiber route for a curtain, you will need a liner.
- For built-up soap scum use melamine sponges (Mr. Clean Magic Eraser or the generic equivalent.)

In summary, the bathroom is important in feng shui and in your quest for a better life as your health and wellbeing, as well as family finances (!) are tied to this room. After the bedroom, this is the room where your day begins and ends; make it a bright and healthy place.

11

Creating Your Own Personal Sanctuary

Hectic commute to and from work? Kids fighting over who gets the remote? Does the dog need to be walked? Is the telephone ringing off the hook with telemarketers? Calgon take us all away! We all need a little pampering to help deal with the stresses and anxieties of our life and to help maintain peace of mind. But how do you do this, when you share your space with a roommate, a husband, kids, pets, and/or parents? Believe it or not, you can create our own personal sanctuary where you can have your "Calgon moment." It's easier than you think.

There are actually three different ways or places you can create a personal sanctuary (PS). The first is an inner sanctuary, or "your happy place." This has been a mantra for years to help get away from a stressful situation. My personal favorite is lying in a hammock on the beach with Jimmy Buffet music playing, and watching the ocean waves roll onto the sand…ahhhhhh…I feel better already! The nice thing about this PS is that it can be with us all of the time. But how do we build this inner sanctuary? Sit back in a quiet place when you have some alone time. You only need about 20–30 minutes. Close your eyes and relax. Now, bring up the image of your ideal spot for a retreat. It might be the mountains, a forest stream, a church, or a romantic B&B…There are no right or wrong places here. Enter this retreat and see your special place. It can be a hammock, a rock next to the stream, or a big comfortable bed. Pick whatever and wherever you need to feel totally comfortable and stress-free. What do you see or hear? What are the textures? Really immerse yourself.

Some meditation experts suggest bringing another person into your PS as a sounding board for your dreams, worries and fears. This person can be living, dead or fictional (i.e. a parent, a religious figure, a political figure…)

Your inner PS is now complete, ready to be called upon when you need to escape to "your happy place."

The second type of PS is the physical sanctuary of your home. This space can be your entire house if you live alone, or a room, or a corner that contains your favorite chair or the bathtub (for an uninterrupted ½ hour soak.) If you share your space with others, it is imperative that your privacy and theirs, when a retreat is needed, is respected. When you are in your personal sanctuary, you can read, write, listen to music or meditate…do whatever brings you a sense of peace and calm.

If you are lucky enough to be able to takeover a room for your personal sanctuary, you might consider one of the two most popular rooms-the bathroom and the bedroom. These rooms are associated with rest, relaxation and rejuvenation. Let's start with the bathroom.

In history, the bath was a ceremony for purifying the body and soul. Essential oils, herbs and plants were used to complete the cleansing experience. We've lost this feeling of "ceremony" in our hustle and bustle world, which is sad. There is nothing more centering and relaxing than a hot bath, some lit candles, soft music playing and a glass of wine to forget the world beyond the bathroom door. Although this isn't practical on a daily basis, you do need to take time on a weekly basis to truly pay attention to your body, as it is the vehicle in which you live your life. Stress manifests itself physically in the form of headaches, stomach-aches, insomnia, depression, fatigue and, even worse, heart problems. So use stress relief as your excuse to lock the door, crank some music, indulge in expensive soaps and lotions and sing at the top of your lungs, or maybe just relax with a glass of wine and some candles and forget the outside world.

Here are some tips to transform the bathroom into a place for your mind, body and spirit:

- Incorporate all five senses and elements in your design scheme. Color, scent and sound are very important in creating your personal sanctuary. Use a cool color scheme to promote rest and relaxation, soothing scents to calm and transport you to your "happy place" and sounds to help complete the transition.

- Soundproof the space as much as possible to prevent household noises from intruding into the space (or from inside noises, like your singing, from being heard outside.) You can also consider replacing the door with a solid core wood door, which can reduce noise transmittal by up to 50%, to really give you the sense of being "away."

- Lighting is a key factor to help set the mood. You definitely don't want the harsh, bright lights on you that you would use to put on make-up or shave when you're trying to forget the fight you had with a co-worker in your PS. As discussed in the bathroom chapter, you need multi-levels of lighting for proper make-up application so there are no shadows. That being said, overhead lighting is too harsh for your sanctuary. Soft, natural light from a window, tinted light bulbs or candles are the ways to create an intimate, sensuous environment.

The goal of making the bathroom your personal sanctuary is to replicate a spa experience without the price tag or hassle and stress of getting there!

The bedroom is the next room to consider for a personal sanctuary. The bedroom is my favorite room to design. It is the room where you begin and end each and every one of your days. It sets the tone, albeit subconsciously, for all of your interactions with others including yourself (remember your self-talk.) For many, though, the bedroom is merely a functional space and is usually the last one to be decorated. For me, it's the first and most important room in the house. This room, by definition, should be the ultimate sanctuary for rest and relaxation. And isn't that what the room is for?

Unfortunately, most bedrooms are no longer just for sleeping. They have become multi-tasking, multi-use spaces resulting in sleep becoming a secondary concern. Kid's bedrooms are used for entertaining friends, studying, dressing and sleeping, and are usually in a 10x10 space. Master bedrooms are turned into home offices, exercise rooms, dressing rooms, a place for romance, and oh yeah, sleeping. Designing children and teens' rooms is an art in and of itself, so when speaking of personal sanctuaries, I am referring mainly to the master bedroom. However, some of the tips can be used for a child's space when appropriate.

A sanctuary, by definition, should transport you to another place and time to relax and recharge your batteries. Sleeping is your body's way of regenerating from the abuse you put it through on a daily basis. It is something you must do to properly get through the day. You must take back your bedroom as a space for sleeping. The bedroom is for two activities: sleep and romance-period. It is not a place for working, exercising or watching TV. Here are some tips for taking back the bedroom:

- De-clutter: Revisit the clutter chapter. There should be nothing under the bed as this, in feng shui terms, causes you to sleep on unresolved issues. From a health standpoint, the "under-bed" clutter impedes proper air circulation around you.

- Excessive electronic gadgets in the bedroom, or any room, are troubling from a health aspect due to the high levels of EMFs being emitted into the space. This excess of electricity in the room can disrupt your sleep patterns and in some cases/studies, it has been shown to adversely affect your health contributing to higher rates of cancer, migraines and fatigue. Phones and clocks, which are necessities in a bedroom, should be kept an average of three feet away from the headboard of the bed. Keeping the clock further away will also prevent you from abusing your snooze button! I've had many people disagree with me about having a TV and computer in the room stating they "need to have the TV on to fall asleep" or "there's no other place for the computer." If you are in an apartment or small home and this is a valid complaint, I suggest a closed entertainment center to close the doors when the TV is not in use. There are also closed desk units that can be used to "hide work" when you are transitioning the bedroom from a work to sleep environment.

- The color scheme should be in cool colors to help lower heart rate and blood pressure and to promote good sleep. You sleep better in a cool space. Think blues, purples and greens. If you want to add some "excitement" for a romantic evening, bring red and pink in as accents. This might include candles, pillows or a throw.

- Utilize your power position to feel psychologically secure in the bedroom space.

- You spend 1/3 of your life sleeping. Make sure it's quality sleep with as high a quality mattress that you can afford. This goes for bed linens as well. Go for a high thread count in the sheets for that soft, luxurious feel that makes you want to get into bed!

Now that you've got the room set up for sleeping, how do you add the touches to make it a sanctuary? Here are some ideas to help you:

- First, think sanctuary. Go back to your inner sanctuary and try to recreate the same environment here. That doesn't mean you have to turn your bedroom into a Tiki hut if you like the beach (you can if you're extreme, but typically not recommended,) however, you can bring in the color scheme of the beach into the space. Consider an Art Deco color scheme if

Miami is a favorite, the deep turquoise and white of Greece or the various shades of blues, turquoise and greens of the Caribbean. Bring in the textures of the beach: sand in a jar to hold votive candles, shells, grass cloth wall coverings, linen for draping on the windows and bed…

- Just as in the bathroom, make this space as healthy as possible by choosing natural materials for bedding, mattress, any scents you bring into the space and the curtains.

- Lighting is key here as well. Your general light is usually a ceiling light or fan. The lights can be on a dimmer to create whatever atmosphere you want. Whether it is: dressing, sleeping or romance…Task lighting also needs to be addressed. Place an extra table lamp on a dresser, nightstand or by your jewelry case so you grab the right color socks or earrings. Who hasn't fallen into that trap? Accent lighting can also be used to highlight collections, pieces of furniture or artwork.

***This is your sanctuary, your place away from the rest of the world. Remove the photos of your kids, friends and parents. This space is for relaxation and romance. Put the other pictures in social spaces and only place photos of you and your significant other in this room. ***

Other rooms and spaces can also be used for your personal sanctuary. A rarely used guestroom, a converted attic or a corner in your home office can all be claimed for your alone time. It must be re-iterated, especially if you can't claim a room for your own, that when you are in "your space" that your privacy is to be respected. You can have some fun and make your own "Do Not Disturb" sign to really get the point across! In your corner, utilize the applicable aforementioned tips, but also apply your own accessories to personalize "your space." Have your special blanket draped over a comfy chair to curl up with when reading. Have a favorite mug for coffee when contemplating life and your MP3 player filled with your favorite tunes to really transport you to a different place and time when journaling. Earphones are a great way to really ensure your privacy, as it is easier to ignore distractions when you can't hear them.

When accessorizing your PS, again, refer to the chapter on clutter. If you don't love it or need it in your space, don't include it. Accessorize your PS with things that will inspire you to create or that will motivate you. It doesn't matter if others don't feel the same way as you do; this is your space and your space alone. Here is where you can showcase your collections or passions. Do you have a bright fuchsia blanket that your husband hates? Put it here. Hang your spoon collection here or stack your beloved books. A true retreat is a celebration of you and your passions.

*** *A personal sanctuary doesn't have to be inside your home. It can be a park, place of worship, library or museum.* ***

Another place to create a personal sanctuary is the outdoors. Select a place in a garden or yard where you can find peace. If you chose somewhere outside on your property for your PS, the same rules apply. Select a comfortable piece of furniture (hammock!) lighting (if outside at night, candles, torches,) sound (fountain, chimes, music, natural sounds of wildlife) and accessories (garden figurines/ statues, flowers/landscaping.) I always feel recharged when spending time outside, no matter what the weather is. Watching my two dogs playing in the snow, just laying in the sun, and experiencing all of the wildlife that calls my yard their home, rejuvenates me. Just soaking up whatever sun I can seems to be just what the doctor ordered on some days. Nature is truly the perfect unprescribed form of Prozac!

If you are truly motivated, and have a bit of a green thumb, you can create a healing garden or a Zen garden as your personal sanctuary. Many hospitals and hospices are incorporating healing gardens on their grounds for their patients, patient's family and staff to use. When creating these spaces, remember to incorporate all elements into the design-a water feature is key. It can be a fountain or a small pond that can also help to mask unwanted sounds. A comfortable place to sit, whether it's a bench, chair or the ground, will add to the experience and help if you will be sitting for long periods in meditation.

Romy Rawlings states in her book *Healing Gardens,* "…we should learn to think of…(gardens)…as a haven where we can be embraced by the natural world." Wow, that puts it in perspective. Rawlings goes on to say that "the garden is a perfect place for self expression, a place where you can be creative, developing aspects of your self that may be denied elsewhere in your life." You can easily add color and humor to a garden through your flower/plant choices and what you choose to accent your garden with. Do you have gnomes, angels or butterfly figurines placed throughout? Let your personality shine.

Finding time to visit your personal sanctuary, whether it's your inner, physical or outer sanctuary is critical in balancing the demands your life places upon you, or that you place upon it. You must take the time to recharge by getting a good night's sleep, having some alone time or time to just "be." Get lost in a daydream or unleash your inner Picasso. This time is as essential to your wellbeing as food, water, and breathing is in maintaining a healthy body, mind and spirit.

12

Maintain a Smooth flow of Energy throughout your Space-Being the Traffic Controller of Your Home

Slow, meandering paths throughout your house…what? This chapter is basic space-planning 101. In a nutshell, if you are constantly bumping into the entertainment center as you round a corner-MOVE IT! Bruising your knee is not considered good feng shui. Think about it. You are mad as you now have sharp pain emanating throughout your body, resulting in a bruise. Whenever you see the bruise or pass by the offending entertainment center, you automatically tense up as you remember the pain. Then you get angry, thereby creating negative energy in the space and affecting your day. This can negatively affect your interactions with others throughout the day. Wow, just from bumping your knee. Does this sound a little extreme? Maybe, but you get the point.

Straight lines in feng shui are called "poison arrows" and are, in fact, a conduit of energy. Since the line or path is straight, the energy moves fast and hits directly whatever is in its path. From a psychological standpoint, this is unsettling. You can never fully relax if you are sitting in this position. An example of this is a reception desk directly in line with the front door. You should never situate someone here, but rather off to the side. In many home floor plans, there is typically a bedroom that sits at the end of a hallway with two side halls off to either side leading to additional bedrooms. This causes a "T-junction." The person who sleeps in this room, in most cases, suffers from restless sleep, headaches and is generally more irritable than the rest of the family.

To remedy this, you can hang crystals or other items from the ceiling (i.e. wind chimes, fabric or interesting light fixtures) to attract the eye up and to effectively slow down energy flow. Hanging detailed artwork on the walls also works. Pick pictures that require you to stop and look closely at what is being shown. Think of the popular family gallery walls in most homes. You stop and look (and laugh) to see what is going on in the picture. Detailed runners or area rugs in a hallway also help to direct and slow down energy movement throughout the space.

***Never purchase a home or locate your business at the end of a T-junction. It can be dangerous, as there can be damage if someone runs the stop sign. ***

Another "poison arrow" situation can occur with the outside walk leading to your home. If the path is a straight shot from the sidewalk/street to your door, you can "cure" this poison arrow with landscaping. Plant bushes, flowers or plants that spread. Hostas are the perfect plant for this, and they seem to grow anywhere! In my opinion, hostas are the aspirin plant of nature.

Now, stand inside your front door, and as stated in the chapter on entryways, look around you. If you can see directly to the back of the home and out a door or window, you have a problem. Energy, and opportunity is coming in just fine, but like the stairway from the upper level, it's going right on out again. To help solve this issue, see what you can do to block the view of the back of the house. This can be as easy as placing a crystal or sun catcher in the window at the back of the house or re-arranging some furniture, so the path isn't a straight line. Plants, fabric and runners can also help to direct traffic throughout the space.

All right, now you've gotten rid of poison arrows, but how do you make sure your rooms are set up right? A great exercise is to make a floor plan of each room of your house. Place the large pieces of furniture and mark windows and any doorways. Next, take a pencil and, starting at the front door, draw a line throughout the space from room to room without taking your pencil off of the paper. You will be surprised at what you "bump into" or the windows you'll run through. You probably won't even be conscious of the furniture you've been stepping over, bumping into or moving around for all these years.

Furniture groupings should be open to the doorway for those entering the room to be "welcomed" to the conversations. A U-shaped pit group in front of a fireplace is not a welcome grouping. Rather, a perpendicular grouping of two sofas or a sofa and two chairs is fine as you can "enter the group from the top." A furniture grouping should also be anchored with an area rug. An area rug keeps the grouping from floating in the space, especially if one of the pieces of the grouping is not against a wall.

While this is a rather hard concept to understand, the barriers (i.e. the furniture) that you put up, and the pathways throughout your space does affect you and your sense of security. Think of yourself as the "traffic controller" in your home or office. Direct all occupants, guests and energy where you want them to go. You don't want to do all this "decorating" and have people/energy enter through the front door and right on through the back door. Being aware of the traffic patterns in your home will create an open, calming and secure space that will help balance all of your life areas.

13

Bringing Creativity Back in Your Life

Creativity is a frequently mentioned topic. Be more creative! Think outside of the box! What box you may ask? What does it mean to be creative? Let's discuss what needs to be present in your environment for you to be creative and why being creative is important to you when designing the life of your dreams.

The thought and theory of creativity is so important that studies have shown that "creativity and innovation" are listed at the top of lists of business functions that companies most valued in their employees. This was reinforced in a study done for the Entrepreneurship Initiative at the University of Strathclyde in Scotland of over 100 small to medium sized businesses. The "value of creative work in an economy that is driven by information and rapid change is now rarely disputed," writes Kim McManus, PhD in her paper *On Becoming Creative*. McManus goes on to say, "My argument and my hope are that with genuine effort and some luck, the creative process may become a lifelong outlet for any individual's self-expression and personal fulfillment." Amen.

***Creativity is not just for the Stephen Kings, Picassos and Steven Spielbergs of the world. Remember, they all had to start somewhere too! ***

I think the biggest block to creativity is the fear of making a mistake, or being laughed at because our idea isn't perfect. My answer to that is WHO CARES! Esther Hicks wrote in her book *Ask and It Is Given* that we must "remove the trees from our path" to create the life we desire. What are "the trees" you ask? The trees are our inner critic, who can be ruthless, or "well-meaning" friends and family who are "just looking out for our best interests." The trees ask, "Who do you think you are?" or "You're not good enough" (or rich enough, or pretty enough…) or the dreaded "but what if you fail?" Well, what if you do fail? What is the worst thing that could happen? You waste a few pieces of paper writing down your thoughts on a story idea, or you spend an hour drawing or doodling…so what? You actually may find out you're good at something.

There are very few people who accomplish perfection in anything the first time out. For 99% of us, it takes practice, focus, passion and desire. So to quit something after the first try or worse, to stop before you even try, is sad.

Sheryl Crow sings "*if it makes you happy, it can't be that bad…*" and she's right. (The qualifier is, that as long as what makes you happy isn't illegal or immoral, then it really can't be all that bad.) You may not be able to write the great American novel or get $1 million for a movie screenplay. However, you might publish one of your poems, one of your photos may be part of a charity calendar, or you may follow your passion and open a small store that capitalizes on your life-long passion for baseball cards. But…you'll never know unless you try.

So, how do you get over your fear of failure, or being imperfect? How do you gather the courage to cut down "the trees?" You must first give yourself permission to be imperfect and make a mistake. Easy, right? However, in a society that conditions you from birth that if you aren't a certain height, or weight, you "aren't attractive enough," or don't make $50K by the time you're 30, "you're a failure in your career." Being imperfect is scary. Me, I've turned imperfection into an art form. I'm the one in my group of friends who isn't afraid "to make a fool of herself" by trying a new hair color, taking a class (sometimes by myself) or starting my own business. In all, I've really had only one BAD hair color that I cried over, and I've learned some great new things on some offbeat topics. More importantly, I have a career that I like and makes me happy. (Why isn't everyone doing this?) But to do these things, I had to give myself permission to be imperfect and know that "it might not turn out the way I want it to." I also had to get over the fear of what others "would think" about attending a class by myself or striking out on my own in the business world. What I've learned along the way is that sometimes it turns out BETTER than you expect it to. I've met some very interesting people. I'm great at small talk and getting interesting conversations started (how many people do you know who can explain the history of Feng Shui?) and I'm traveling and teaching a topic that I'm passionate about. If you have an inkling to try something you've never done before, do it. You never know what lies around the corner!

There are three conditions that must exist in an individual for creativity to flourish. They are openness to the experience, an internal focus of evaluation and the ability to toy with concepts. Let's discuss being "open to the experience"—letting go of having to be perfect and enjoying the journey. This is a "loosening of the boundaries that establish our sense of reality-our beliefs, perceptions, biases (i.e. If you don't look like Heidi Klum you're doomed to singledom forever) at any given time" states McManus. Creativity flourishes in the possibility of "what ifs." What if you paint a wall apple green-it will accent the green in the sofa.... What if you take a class on speaking Spanish-you'll learn a valuable skill for your business, be able to speak to others on your next vacation, or you may get a date with the cute guy sitting next to you! Enjoy the present and the journey...you may never want to reach the destination.

McManus continues, "...The most fundamental condition of creativity is that the source or focus of evaluative judgment is internal. The value of his product is, for the creative person, established not for the praise of criticism of others, but by himself." Therefore, it takes some confidence to be creative. It takes a sense of self and ability to try no matter what the consequences. You need to allow yourself the freedom from "restrictions of external evaluation" or "the trees."

Carl Rogers, PhD writes in his observations that "creativity flourishes under conditions of psychological safety where the individual is accepted and valued apart from what they produce, where external evaluation is absent..." McManus weighs in on this by stating, "Feedback from others is not dismissed...rather, it is of primary importance, BUT with an empathetic understanding...internal standards." So, you can take others advice and opinions into consideration but no one can really say what is right for you, as they haven't experienced your life experiences, thoughts and feelings. You can only follow your heart and go from there.

***If you're going to dream about doing, being or getting something fabulous ...DREAM BIG. If you're going to do it, you might as well do it up right! ***

The ability to toy with elements and concepts "might be less important than the first two...." writes Rogers, but "associated with the openness and lack of rigidity described...is the ability to play spontaneously with ideas, colors, shapes, relationships...to express the ridiculous, to translate form one form to another.... It is from this spontaneous toying and exploration that there arises the hunch, the creative seeing of life in a new and significant way." So, if someone tells you only a square table will work in a space, or you must have a dust ruffle, or you must always paint your ceiling white, know that there are other options and that there are few things in life that are so tragic that they can't be fixed.

OK-so how do you encourage creativity in your life? Here's how:

- Encourage the flow of stimulating information.
- Ensure informational feedback whenever possible and as quickly as possible.
- Provide new experiences and create sources of information.
- Process whatever learning occurs.
- Share stories of successes and failures.
- Tolerate mistakes as inevitable when learning through the experiences of trail and error.

So how does this apply to design? Easy. Most people I work with are afraid of color. They ask, "What if I don't like it once it's painted?" Guess what…paint is inexpensive and can be painted over if an area doesn't turn out quite like you anticipated. A pain, yes, but not a tragedy. In fact, painting a wall the wrong color is such a fear that Benjamin Moore has created 2 oz. paint samples that you can "try out" on the wall and live with for a week before you commit to the color. Color is important in feng shui and design. It's been demonstrated that color can affect us mentally, emotionally and physically, so why not embrace it?

***Painting is an investment of a $20 can of paint and a few hours of your time. You might find out that you are a RED person after-all. ***

The very nature of design is being creative. Design is the creation of something NEW that will help fill a need, fix a "room usage" problem or create a new atmosphere. Do you think DaVinci went with his first draft of the Mona Lisa? No, he worked on it (as he did all of his works) continuously…a highlight here; a shade there-until the patron demanded the item that was paid for. But do you see the imperfection he saw? No, you only see some of history's greatest masterpieces and inventions that were so far ahead of his time, that we are only now appreciating his genius some 500+ years later. So you see, creativity AND PERFECTION is in the eye of the beholder.

Lastly, in your quest for creativity, you must not get caught up in the seriousness of "being creative" and the labels society will place upon you. You're "a writer."

You're "an artist." You're "creative." Be playful and have fun with your creativity. This will make it easier to be imperfect or to fail. (Failure being defined as "not turning out as YOU want it to.") Laugh and enjoy your imperfection. Think of the doors that will open by your being "imperfect." You'll meet new people at the craft store, you'll learn a new skill (I learned how to lay a tile floor on one of my missions) or, God forbid, you'll find a hidden talent that you didn't know you had.

14

Detoxing Your Space's Space

Did you know that the air you breathe inside your house is more polluted than the air you breathe outside? In fact, the EPA considers poor air quality a top risk to human health. Indoor air is three times more polluted than outdoor air. But DeAnna, you're thinking, I live in a quiet suburb not near a factory, so how can my air be bad? Carpeting, paint, household cleaners, fabrics, even the candles you light for ambience are all culprits in polluting your indoor air. Many of these things were created to make your life easier, however, they also give off vapors or volatile organic compounds (VOCs) which can cause allergies (or make existing ones worse,) compromise respiratory problems, cause headaches and make life miserable for those with environmental sensitivities.

Over the last 30+ years, houses and office buildings have been constructed with energy conservation in mind. Doors fit tighter, if they open at all, and window drafts are a thing of the past! At the same time, a new wave of chemicals have been invented and injected into building materials, cleaners and household supplies. There are about 75,000 chemicals being used in everything from carpet pads to dryer sheets, window cleaners, dish soaps, hair products, air fresheners, bedding, aromatherapy products and pet supplies.

We talked previously about off gassing, but what exactly does it mean? Molecules break down and pollute the stale air inside our tightly sealed homes and offices. People often complain about "canned, dead air" inside airplanes, sick building syndrome at offices, or colds passed back and forth between family members. According to the National Institute of Health, we are "marinating in a broth of invisible toxins that cause everything from headaches to cancers."

*** *The best way to get rid of "dead" air-open a window! Even in winter, opening a window or door for even a few minutes will help clear the dust and energize a space and it's occupants.* ***

What's one of the simplest least expensive ways to clean the air in your home? Plants. In fact, one of the best ways to breathe clean air in your home is to have one plant for every 100 square feet of space. Plants clean the air by breathing in dirty air and trapping pollutants, and then expelling oxygen-rich clean air. Substances such as formaldehyde, benzene and ammonia (the afore-mentioned VOCs) are transformed, while keeping humidity levels steady. This in turn helps to keep allergies at bay. "If you are bothered by mold, stop it from growing by putting an inch of aquarium gravel on top of the potting soil. This will also help stop cats from digging in there as well," states Avery Hurt in his article *Freshen the Air* from the March, 2006 issue of Better Homes and Gardens.

Although any kind of plant is beneficial, some plants do a better job of cleaning the air than others. They are known to be easy to grow and tough to kill. Fortunately, many of the best plants for cleaning the air also are traditional household favorites. These are a few:

Bamboo palm	Boston fern
Rubber Plant	Peace Lily
Spider Plant	Corn Plant
English ivy	Janet Craig dracaena

Did you realize that candles are one of the biggest indoor air polluters because of the materials they are made of, scented with and the prevalent use of lead-based metal wicks? If you burn a candle with a lead wick, every time it burns the lead is deposited on the walls, furniture and floors. Even these low levels of lead exposure can lead to lack of coordination, low-level fatigue and behavioral disorders. In 1973, the US Consumer Product Safety Commission asked candle manufacturers to replace lead wicks with zinc. However, compliance is voluntary and often not checked. It is up to you, the consumer, to be informed and make smart purchasing decision. The best choice for wicks is an organic, unbleached cotton wick.

*** *Australia succeeded in banning lead wicks in 1999.* ***

Did you know that paraffin is a petroleum by-product obtained from oil refineries, and there are at least seven toxins (including benzene) in paraffin? Most fragrance oils used in candle making are also petroleum based. There are some good options however; candles are now made of palm wax, soy and beeswax. Also, when purchasing a scented candle, or any other aromatherapy product, look for items scented with essential oils and botanicals. These candles are available at most locations that sell this type of product. You may pay a little more, but these candles tend to last longer, have a longer lasting scent and don't cause the sooting, smoking and blackening that can occur with their paraffin, fragrance-scented alternatives. If an item is tagged with the line "fragrance" the scent is a synthetic, man-made creation. Buying a "healthy" candle is as simple as reading the ingredient label. If you can't pronounce the ingredients, back away from the candle.

OK, so you've cleaned the air of toxins, but what about dust? What's the best way to deal with it? Heloise, from *Hints from Heloise* advises to keep dust at a minimum by first vacuuming it away and then using a micro fiber cloth to pick up the residuals, even on fabric surfaces. Just doing basic maintenance on your HVAC unit will also help. Change the disposable filter on your A/C unit monthly and frequently vacuum it if your filter is reusable. Another great tip to cut down on dust and dirt in your home is to have walk-off mats at each door, and remember to take off your shoes upon entering your home. I have some clients who keep a basket of slippers at the entrance for their guests once they are shoe-less.

We are living in the most technologically advanced time in our history. But what is the price we're paying for all of this information, data, music and convenience? Electric and magnetic fields (EMFs) and the AC electric and magnetic fields surround us and disrupt our nervous systems. The AC electric field emanates from most appliances, whether they are turned on or not. The AC magnetic field originates from the current radiating from water and gas pipes, ungrounded household wiring, appliances and high-voltage lines. These electric fields have been shown to cause everything from insomnia to chronic fatigue and leukemia.

In terms of décor and design, how can you make a difference? Barrie Gillies wrote in the article, *What can you do about the Environment?*, that by taking "small steps, we actually make a difference." I agree. With gas prices hitting all-time highs and healthcare costs growing increasingly unaffordable, it makes sense to be pro-active in creating healthy working and residential spaces. Whenever possible, use environmentally responsible paint, textiles and wall coverings. Do your research, and when in doubt ASK.

***A typical 3-bedroom home being built today can have more than 2,000 pounds of petrochemical products incorporated in the construction materials. This includes: car-*

pet, paint, mastics, wire insulation, laminate flooring, foam sheathing, weather strip-
ping, PVC sewer and vents, flexible duct systems, additives and bonding agents. ***

As previously stated, paint can off-gas VOCs (volatile organic compounds) into
your space. VOCs, considered essential until recently, include benzene and formaldehyde. They have been shown to cause headaches, nausea, dizziness and eye,
throat and ear problems. Anyone who has painted a room has experienced any
one, if not all of these, when proper ventilation wasn't available. When buying
paint, you want something that contains low or no VOCs. Most paint manufacturers make this type, but you must ask for it. Oil-based paints off-gas more than
water-based or latex paint.

*** *The EPA has classified formaldehyde as a probable carcinogen. This toxin is found*
in clothing, draperies, paint, and any permanently pressed fabric and carpeting.
Formaldehyde is a pungent smelling gas that can cause watery eyes, nausea, breathing
difficulties and trigger asthma attacks. ***

Great strides have been made in the manufacturing of fabric. Paper, recycled soda
bottles, straw, wool and tires are just a few examples of recycled materials being
made into fabric. When in doubt, look for naturals: cotton, wool and the like. A
note should be made when buying anything cotton. The cotton industry is noto-
rious for its use of pesticides in the growing and cleaning process. Look for NAT-
URAL or ORGANIC labels when making this purchase. Cotton is also bleached
to make it pristine white. If you have any sort of environmental sensitivity or are
prone to allergies or other upper respiratory illnesses, stay away from the bleach.
All of this information is listed on the label.

Wall coverings are also being created from natural and recycled materials, and
printed with water-soluble inks containing no metals. When purchasing wall coverings, look for these options, as they will help your walls "breathe" and decrease
the chance for mold/mildew build-up. They also help with room ventilation. It
should also be noted, that you can get low or no VOC adhesives/glues and water
soluble application products to put up your wall coverings. It would defeat the
purpose to buy a natural wall covering, only to apply it with an adhesive that will
off-gas into the space. Check with a sustainable builder or designer in your area
or visit the Healthy Home or GAIAM websites where these products are also
available for purchase.

While carpet provides a visually pleasing floor covering and adds warmth and cushion underfoot, extra care must go into its purchase. Although I personally enjoy the look and feel of a hardwood floor, because it's easy to maintain and is pet-friendly, there are some good carpet options. Eco-friendly carpets, adhesives and carpet pads, made of recycled plastics, are available. Carpeting can off-gas up to three years after installation! Take care to minimize this risk if you must have wall-to-wall carpeting. Remember, most carpeting is made of man-made synthetic fibers that have gone through a major manufacturing process in its creation, not to mention all of the color, stain guarding and anti-static products that are added.

Before you lay down your new wall-to-wall carpet remember to thoroughly vacuum your EXISTING carpet before it gets pulled up. You will be amazed at the amount of dust and dirt that is trapped in the fibers, and will be released into the air (even if you vacuum regularly.) It is also OK to ask the carpet retailer to unroll your newly purchased carpet in a well-ventilated area BEFORE installation. If possible, make sure the room is well ventilated up 48 hours during and after installation.

Green Carpets	*Conventional Carpet*
Natural fibers	Synthetic fibers
Low VOCs	High VOCs
Naturally stain resistant	Spray-on stain resistant chemicals
Natural jute backing	Synthetic rubber backing
Lower toxicity	Potentially high toxicity

When deciding on what flooring to put into your home, evaluate your lifestyle. Do you have pets and kids? If so, do you really want to be vacuuming every day? Does anyone in the home have allergies or any other upper respiratory ailments? Do you entertain often? If you answer yes to any of these questions, you may want to look at hard flooring options and get area rugs to add warmth and color to the room. If you are having problems finding a particular size, color or pattern of area rug, you can have any style of "wall-to-wall" carpeting custom cut and bound for you. Ask for pricing on this option at any carpet retailer.

Hard flooring options include: bamboo, any other hardwood, tile, marble, terrazzo or limestone, just to name a few. While the initial costs may be higher than other types of flooring, in the long run these materials are cost effective as well as environmentally responsible. You are installing a longer-lasting material than traditional carpet that can end up in a landfill when replaced. Nationwide, about 4 billion tons of carpet and padding end up in landfills EVERY YEAR!

****When replacing your old, worn-out carpet, ask what the retailer's carpet reclamation program is. Some carpet manufacturers recycle old carpet instead of dumping it into landfills.* ***

OK, so you've decided to pull up all of your wall-to-wall carpeting and install a hardwood floor, but how do you keep that beautiful hardwood floor from becoming dull? Easy-black tea. Steep the tea and let it cool to room temperature, then use a mop or soft cloth, ring out and wipe onto floor. Used dryer sheets are also great in picking up stray hairs and dust. Be warned though NOT to use a fresh dryer sheet as this can leave a mark.

****Instead of air freshener, fill your home with the fresh scent of spring, even in FALL. Sprinkle dried lavender on floors and carpets before vacuuming. The lavender's natural oils will heat up and circulate in the vacuum and air.* ***

In terms of buying natural or organic household cleaners, it isn't always as easy as it sounds. Unless you make your own cleaners and bath/body products, you are at the mercy of manufacturers and ingredient lists that you may or may not be able to decipher. Some of the more commonly used chemicals and where they can be found are as follows:

- Methylene chloride, known to cause cancer in animals is found in paint strippers, adhesive removers and aerosol spray paints.

- Benzene, a known human carcinogen, is commonly found in paint supplies.

- Perchloroethlene is an organic compound used in dry cleaning. This toxin is linked to cancer, birth defects and damage to the central nervous system. If you have your clothes dry cleaned, first look for a natural or green cleaners. If one is not in your area, immediately take off the plastic bag that your clothes come home in and air out the clothes. Do not put these clothes back in your closet without airing them out as the dry-cleaning chemicals can get on your other pieces of clothing.

****If you would like to view a listing of safe household products that you can easily find in your local grocery or hardware store see the "Fact Sheet: Safe Substitutes at*

Home: Non-toxic Household Products" *at* http://es.epa.gov/techinfo/facts/safe-fs.html. ***

Here is a suggested cleaning schedule to keep your home clean and healthy:

<u>Daily</u>

- Review mail, magazines and catalogs. Touch paper only once. Throw out junk mail instantly, shred what needs to be shredded and file bills.
- Do the dishes, clean off kitchen counters and stove, wipe out sinks.
- Take out trash.
- Sweep or vacuum floors in kitchen, entry and other high traffic areas: especially if you have children and/or pets.
- Encourage the whole family to hang up clothes/coats and to put away toys.
- Make the beds.

<u>Weekly</u>

- Vacuum the whole house.
- Dust/polish the furniture.
- Do laundry and iron immediately.
- Empty all wastebaskets and recycle old newspapers and magazines.
- Wash the kitchen floor.
- Clean the mirrors you use most often and those in public areas. This is especially important from a feng shui standpoint to bring in positive light and positive energy.
- Change the bedding on beds.

<u>Annually</u>

- Wash curtains, blinds and shades.
- Wash all windows.
- Sort clothes.
- Vacuum radiators and heat ducts.

- Wash bedspreads, slipcovers and blankets. Again, if you have pets and they are allowed on the furniture, wash as often as needed.

- Shampoo carpets, turn rugs to equalize wear on both sides, wash area rugs.

No discussion of "de-toxing" your space would be complete without bringing up mold and it's affects on all occupants. The easiest way to make sure you don't have a mold problem is to control the humidity level of your home. A relative humidity level of 30–50% is generally recommended for residential homes. Eliminate any standing water in and around your home or any generally wet surfaces, because these environments are breeding grounds for mold, mildew, bacteria and insects. Some simple tips to help reduce conditions for mold build-up are:

- Vent your clothes dryer outside.

- Install and use exhaust fans in the kitchen and bathroom that are vented outside.

- Ventilate attics and crawl spaces to prevent moisture build-up.

- Repair any leaks and seepage.

- Thoroughly clean and dry water-damaged carpet (within 24 hours if possible) or consider removal and replacement.

- Keep your home clean. House dust mites, pollens and other allergy causing agents can be reduced.

- Take steps to minimize biological pollutants in basements by disinfecting the basement floor drain regularly and operating a dehumidifier to keep relative humidity levels between 30–50%.

- Install HEPA air filters in vacuum cleaners and furnaces to cut down on dust.

- Wash bedding and soft toys frequently in a temperature above 130 degrees Fahrenheit to kill dust mites.

- Clean refrigerator drip pans regularly and make sure the door seals well.

- Replace moldy shower curtains by removing them and putting in wash machine. Better yet, replace with a glass shower door!

- Clean garbage can/pails frequently.

- Scour sinks and tubs as fungi thrive on soap and other films that coat tiles and grout.

Now that you've de-toxed the inside of your home, what about the outside? You need to make this space as hazard-free as possible for your children, pets, guests and yourself. Think about the time and expense you expend to keep your lawn looking green and weed-free. You fertilize, add pesticides and herbicides until there are more chemicals on your lawn than grass seed, and then panic at the first sign of a dandelion. However, in your quest for this perfect, lush lawn, you are putting the health of your family, pets and any unsuspecting wildlife that may cross over the property line at risk. Your yard has become toxic.

- A study at Purdue University found that homeowners who use weed-and-feed type lawn chemicals increased their dog's risk of developing bladder cancer. Cancer rates in dogs have more than doubled in the last 20 years!

- The US Geological Survey regularly finds every type of chemical, particularly week killers, in streams and rivers around neighborhoods. These weed killers contain the chemical 2.4D, which is responsible for many forms of cancers and neurological and immune deficiencies.

- A study conducted by PETA found that golf course superintendents who often apply pesticides and herbicides have a higher risk of developing brain cancer and non-Hodgkin's lymphoma.

- According to the Non-Government Organization, of the 36 pesticides most commonly used by homeowners, 14 are carcinogens, 15 are linked to birth defects, 21 are linked to reproductive defects, 24 are linked with neurotoxicity and 22 are linked with liver and kidney damage.

Whenever the people in my neighborhood have their lawn service come to spray the lawn, I actually have to keep my dogs inside so that they are not exposed to the fumes. My dog Libby has literally collapsed on the ground after walking past yards that had been sprayed. Think about are the signs that are posted after a spraying has taken place that say "Keep children and pets off." Many pesticides have their roots in nerve gas development from WWII!

There are alternatives to keeping your yard looking great without poisoning everything within your property lines. And no, you don't have to install artificial turf! Look for lawn care products that are natural and non-toxic. St. Gabriel Laboratories has a great new line that is Pet Approved and is safe for wildlife as well. The Pro Pet Alliance of Veterinarians has given their seal of approval.

In addition to using nontoxic products, you can incorporate other natural gardening techniques to keep a healthy, beautiful lawn.

- Sow grass in the fall when there is less competition from weeds and the weather is cooler.

- Grow a mixture of grasses that are grown IN YOUR ZONE. Most gardening centers have tags on their plants and seeds listing what can grow in your climate, or in the cases of plants, what would need to be housed over the winter. Zoysia is a great choice for grass, if appropriate for your locale, as it's a spreading perennial grass that grows thickly and maintains lushness with little watering.

- Set your lawnmower blade higher and leave the clippings on the lawn as a form of mulch. I like this, as I hate raking!

- Learn to live with imperfection-that's part of the beauty of nature. A perfect, green lawn that is 1 ½ inches high is not found in nature...

In creating the life of your dreams, de-toxing or cleansing your home and lifestyle is a critical. You have to get rid of all the harmful and unhealthy things that are literally poisoning your life. As in purging your clutter, de-toxing your space helps to create or prepare a clean slate for you to start anew. Kermit the Frog said, "It ain't easy being green." However, with the numerous choices you have in the marketplace, it's never been easier to be green. And in doing so, it's never been easier to create a beautiful and functioning space that's also healthy. Your home, or office, interior can be green AND fabulous. Your family and friends will be "green" with envy!

15

Conclusion

In designing the life of your dreams, you've learned about the adverse affects of clutter on your mental and physical health, how color affects your moods and a little about the ancient Chinese science of Feng Shui and how you can apply it to your life. With all of the information given, the common thread is the focus on what you truly want to achieve and bring into your life. Do you want to focus on your relationship with family and friends? Then your home will be one of comfort, warm colors and items and photos of family friends. Do you want to focus on wealth and abundance? Then accentuate the luxury of furniture, materials (marble, granite, wool carpeting) and any accessory or personal items that represent wealth to you. If health and well-being are priorities, eco-friendly textiles and cleaners should be featured. Feng shui and the Laws of Attraction help prioritize your goals and dreams.

This book has taken you through the perils of clutter and how what you purchase, keep and store says about your life, where you've been and where you're going. What does your "stuff" say about you? Hopefully, your collections are statements as to where you are currently (recent family photos, awards, clothes that fit and are up-to-date) and not reminders of your past (high school football jersey, stuffed animals from your first boyfriend when you were 15.) Remember, clutter from the past equals emotional baggage! Do you really want to carry all that around with you? It's OK to let go of old, out-dated items that no longer serve their original purpose. Donate it to someone who can use it and move forward.

***Georgia O'Keefe wouldn't bring home anything new into her home unless she got rid of something old! Make sure there's room for growth in any space. ***

Creating a personal sanctuary and bringing in the five elements and senses into your design scheme has also been discussed. Everyone needs a place to plan, be, rest and recharge. Personal sanctuaries accomplish that. By bringing in the five elements and senses into the mix, you are engaging all of your senses and participating in the present moment of your life. You need to know where you are and where you've been to plan and forge into where you want to go. Surround yourself with things that make you happy, colors that you love and your favorite blanket to cuddle into when reading your favorite book. Play that Donny Osmond music and sing at the top of your lungs in your personal sanctuary. It's your place to be and create!

***Give yourself permission to really be yourself. Your personal sanctuary allows you to please only one person, and that's you. ***

Basic color concepts were also discussed, including the significance of color and how to apply it properly. You were made aware of the importance of proper space planning to establish a meandering traffic pattern and flow that makes sense to all who enter the space, while maintaining a sense of security by properly applying psychology principles in utilizing power positions. Knowing basic design concepts (what is taught in design school) and then being able to apply them to your space in ways that work for you is key. If your home or office isn't functional for how it's to be utilized and for all occupants, you're uncomfortable and will avoid certain rooms, not entertain, develop illnesses or generally be depressed and not know why. When you feel good in your space, the rest just seems to fall into place.

***A Chinese proverb says, "If we do not change our direction, we are likely to end up where we are headed." When ignorance ends, negligence begins and its antidote is responsibility. Making the choice to educate ourselves and then act on our newfound knowledge is the ethical obligation of every one of us. ***

Lastly, de-toxifying tips were given identifying why this is an important and integral part of creating a new life and home for you. Whether you are expecting a baby, anticipating an elderly parent moving in, suffer from allergies or just want to make a healthy lifestyle change, this information is a great starting point. Your indoor environments are generally in your control, so armed with that knowledge; it makes sense to make smart choices in what you bring home. Even a minor change in what household cleaners you use, or what candles you burn, can make a difference. Read those labels!!

In designing the life of your dreams you learned that it's OK to let go of things that aren't working for you. It's OK to be selfish in terms of wanting to bring more of something-anything-into your life that makes you happy. You can go for that raise, want a better car, write poetry or travel to lands that intrigue you. It's OK to be happy. Once you define what you want and new priorities, you can use feng shui to identify the 9 life areas and where they are located in your space. You can then decide what areas you would like to "activate" and then choose color or the corresponding element to bring into your décor. How much fun is this?

*** *The Law of Attraction states, "That which is like unto itself, is drawn. And so, the essence of whatever you give your attention to is unfolding in your experience. Therefore, there is nothing that you cannot be, do, or have."* ***

Life is stressful enough, your home shouldn't be. Surround yourself with things you love. Reside in an environment that is calming, healthy and supportive. Your entire home should be a personal sanctuary. It should allow each occupant to shine in his or her own way.

So get out your pink blanket your grandma made you, display those autographed baseball cards OR donate the sweater from an ex, toss the broken TV set (you know you'll never use it for parts like you keep telling yourself) and sell the never-used-but-HAD-TO-HAVE bread maker you got for Christmas in 1995. Design the life you want, and were meant to have, by making the outer changes necessary to help facilitate the inner changes. If you are still having doubts as to what "is right and what is wrong" in terms of goal setting, priorities or what job offer to accept, listen to your feelings. Pay attention to your physical reaction upon thinking about a person, place or thing. If you have butterflies of excitement at the prospect of a new car, or smile in anticipation of a date with your new beau, chances are you're making the right choice. However, if chills run up your spine upon meeting a new sales rep or you are looking for the nearest exit at a job interview, chances are you need to take a pass on that opportunity.

*** *Esther Hicks writes in her book Ask and It Is Given, that we should "Pay attention to the way you feel, and deliberately choose thoughts-about everything-that feel good to you when you think them."* ***

Who doesn't want to feel good and be surrounded by things that make them feels safe and supported? Your home should be an extension of your personality and aspirations. By understanding basic space planning, the importance of color and some help from feng shui principles, you can accomplish all of this and design the life of your dreams from the outside in!

16

Bibliography

Allergy-Free Living: How to Create a Health, Allergy-free Home and Lifestyle, Dr. Peter Howarth and Anita Reid, Octopus Publishing Group, London, 2000

Ask and It Is Given, Esther and Jerry Hicks, Hay House Inc., Carlsbad CA, 2004

Feng Shui Dictionary: Everything you Need to Know to Assess your Space, Find Solutions, and Bring Harmony to your Home, Antonia Beattie, Thunder Bay Press, San Diego, 2003

Feng Shui Step by Step: Arranging your Home for Health and Happiness, T. Raphael Simons, Three Rivers Press, New York, 1996

Green Clean: The Environmentally Sound Guide to Cleaning Your Home, Linda Mason Hunter and Mikki Halpin, Melcher Media, New York, 2005

Healing Gardens, Romy Rawlings, Willow Creek Press, Minoqua, 1998

Homes that Heal and Those that Don't, Athena Thompson, New Society Publishers, British Columbia, Canada, 2004

The Complete Book of Color, Suzy Chiazzari, Barnes and Noble Books, New York, 1998

Your Naturally Healthy Home, Alan Berman, St. Martin's Press, London, 2001

978-0-595-39979-6
0-595-39979-7

Printed in the United States
60266LVS00004B/424-441

9 780595 399796